INTERIOR DESIGN

From THE HOME: ITS FURNISHINGS AND EQUIPMENT, 2/e

RUTH MORTON Consultant, Home Economics

Webster Division, McGraw-Hill Book Company

New York   St. Louis   San Francisco   Auckland   Bogotá   Düsseldorf
Johannesburg   London   Madrid   Mexico   Montreal   New Delhi   Panama
Paris   São Paulo   Singapore   Sydney   Tokyo   Toronto

The Illustration Credits on page 388 of this book are an extension of this copyright page.

Editors: Carol Newman, Dan Zinkus
Editing and Styling: Sal Allocco, Mary Naomi Russell
Design: Valerie Scarpa
Production Supervisor: Angela Kardovich

Photo Editor: Suzanne Volkman
Photo Research: Marina Stefan

Library of Congress Cataloging in Publication Data

Morton, Ruth.
   Interior design from The home, its furnishing and equipment.

   Includes index.
   1. Interior decoration.   I. Morton, Ruth.
The home, its furnishing and equipment. II. Title.
NK2110.M68 1979   747'.8'83   78-26393
ISBN 0-07-043426-3

Copyright © 1979, 1970 by McGraw-Hill, Inc. All Rights Reserved. Printed in the United States of America. No part of this publication may be reproduced, stored in a retrieval system, or transmitted, in any form or by any means, electronic, mechanical, photocopying, recording, or otherwise, without the prior written permission of the publisher.
ISBN: 0-07-043426-3

PART 2 INTERIOR DESIGN

CHAPTER 1 The Importance of Interior Design in Our Lives 210

"Life-Styles" and Interior Design • The Psychological Benefits of Interior Design • The Lifetime Values of Interior Design Skills

CHAPTER 2 Color! Color! Color! 220

Basic Facts about Color • Choosing a Color Combination • Identifying and Using Color Schemes • Using Color in a Room

CHAPTER 3 Establishing a Background 238

Planning Floor Treatments • Planning Wall Treatments • Planning Ceiling Treatments • Planning Woodwork Treatments • Shopping for Background Materials • Before Making the Final Decisions

CHAPTER 4 Knowing Furniture 271

Why Furniture Design Changes • Line and Surface • Traditional Furniture • Contemporary Furniture • "Periodless" Upholstered Furniture • Space-saving Furniture • Money-Saving Furniture • Combining Furniture

CHAPTER 5 Buying Furniture 289

Evaluating Furniture According to Quality • Shopping Procedures • Special Dangers in Buying Furniture

CHAPTER 6 Arranging Furniture 303

Start with a Floorplan • Arranging Furniture for Use • Architecture and Furniture Arrangement • Arranging Furniture for Beauty

CHAPTER 7 Fabrics and Window Treatments 323

Function • Architecture • Eye-Appeal • Special Treatments for Problem Windows • Shopping for Window Treatments

CHAPTER 8 Accessories 348

Lamps • Other Practical Accessories • Wall Treatments • Other Decorative Accessories

CHAPTER 9 Tableware and Household Linens 363

Flatware • Dinnerware • Holloware • Glassware • Table Linen • Table Settings • Household Linen

ABOUT THE AUTHOR

Ruth Morton is a consultant and lecturer on home furnishings. A graduate of the Layton School of Art and the University of Minnesota, she is a member of the American Institute of Decorators and has lectured to clubs, on radio and television, and for the University of Wisconsin Extension Division.

Interior Design

part 2

CHAPTER 1

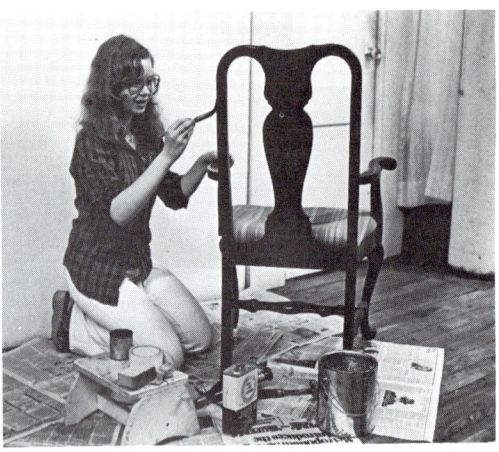

The Importance of Interior Design in Our Lives

Think about your favorite room at home. Picture it in your imagination. Now, ask yourself these questions:

Which piece of furniture in the room is the most comfortable?

Which piece of furniture is the most important?

If you were moving to a different house and could take only one item from this room, what would it be?

If you could change one thing about the room to make it more comfortable, what would you change?

If you could change one thing to make the room more attractive, what change would you make?

If you could buy one new thing to put into the room, what would you buy?

Interior Design Decisions

In answering these questions, you have been trying to make the kinds of decisions that interior designers make professionally. Interior designers are people who select and arrange the various elements that turn an empty space into a useful, comfortable, attractive living area. These elements include furniture, lighting fixtures, floor coverings, fabrics, wall colors, and so on.

This book is designed to help you make similar decisions about furnishing and decorating living spaces. Obviously, learning how to make those decisions is important for anyone who wishes to become an interior designer. The term *interior designer* is a better one than *interior decorator*. A decoration suggests something that is merely added to the surface. A design, on the other hand, suggests a basic overall plan. Design involves how a thing is made and used as well as how it looks. Today, the professionals who plan living spaces are much more concerned with the basics of good design than with mere decoration.

But what if you don't have any plans to become an interior designer? You will still find this book helpful. Sooner or later, each of you will take some responsibility for deciding how your living spaces are to be arranged and how they are to look. Simply moving into a furnished room involves a design decision.

Planning Use of Living Space

In the following chapters, you will learn about the different elements that go into planning the best use of living spaces. Knowing about these elements will help you make design decisions.

If you don't know how to make those decisions effectively, you might agonize over them. You may spend time, energy, and money and not come out with comfort or satisfying beauty. But if you decide wisely, any place in which you live can be excitingly attractive, functionally comfortable, and stimulatingly personal.

In the following chapters, you will have the opportunity to learn the simple but important artistic principles that professional interior designers have gradually worked out through the years. By studying them, you can save yourself from making expensive mistakes. Eventually, you will feel confident enough to take

A well-designed living space is both attractive and functional. The airy openness of this floor-through living area expresses a family's tastes and life-style. Would you feel comfortable here?

Coordinating the fabric of the floor cushions, bedspread, and draperies creates a pleasing, colorful bedroom. Employing a hobby, such as beadwork, as a design element lends a personal, distinctive touch.

the important step of expressing your own individuality and taste in your own surroundings. It is this individuality and personal taste that makes the world interesting!

Which is more important in interior design—artistic principles, or personal taste? Shouldn't you be able to choose a design element simply because you like it?

The answer is that *liking* something is only *one* reason for choosing it. You should never buy something that you do not like. But you should also never buy something only because you like it. Every element in a room, in an apartment or in a house, must do more than merely please the eye. It must do much, much more, in fact. That is what this book is really about. Furnishing and decorating a room is a complex process. Only if you understand the many different elements that go into a successful room design will you be able to begin making choices that you know will be the "right" ones. Then your choices will be right not only for today but for a long time to come.

"LIFE-STYLES" AND INTERIOR DESIGN

The more you know about the way you like to live, the wiser your interior design decisions will be.

How do you like to spend your leisure time? If you enjoy spending hours curled up with a good book, your interior design should include a chair or sofa comfortable enough for long hours of sitting and a bright reading lamp. If you prefer listening to records, you will need to plan for a convenient place for storing your records so that you can use them easily. If you build automobile models or sew your own clothes, you need to plan for storage space and a large work surface in a well-lighted area.

What is Life-style?

How people live, spend free time, entertain friends, and relate to the people with whom they live can be called their life-style. A young couple with no children, with both people holding down full-time jobs, will have a certain life-style. An elderly person who lives alone and does volunteer work at a local hospital three afternoons a week will have another. People living in a house in the country, miles from the nearest shopping center, will have a life-style different from that of people living in an apartment building in a large city. A family in which all members share an interest in outdoor sports will have a life-style different from a family in which each member has individual hobbies and interests.

Trends in Life-style

To be successful, an interior design must take into consideration the life-style of the person or people involved and must provide comfortably for their needs. Let's take a look at some trends in the way people live that affect their choices about living space.

Mobility. One of the most obvious changes in the way we live today as compared with the way people lived fifty years ago is our mobility. Now, few people expect to stay in the same area for their whole lives. Some people move when they finish high school and leave for an out-of-town college. Sometimes, a move is caused by a new job. Occasionally, a person in the same job will be transferred to a different branch or office hundreds or thousands of miles away. Sometimes, a change in marital status causes a major move. A marriage or a divorce may make moving to a different area essential. Of course, a person may move many times within a single city. A young person may move out of the old

---

Energy Tips

In the colder climates, people make use of heavy fabrics, slipcovers, furniture throws, decorative rug hangings, cushions, and throw pillows. In warmer climates, bare wood, straw rugs, woven furniture, and chairs with open spaces are more comfortable. Heavy fabrics and decorative cushioning serve as insulation and save additional heating expenses. Open furniture creates maximum use of natural air conditioning.

Modular or sectional furniture can be used to define or separate living areas in multipurpose spaces.

family home and into an apartment. The next move may be into a larger apartment. Later, there may be another move into a house.

We have become a nation of people on the move. So one question that everyone should keep in mind when selecting furniture is: "Will it travel?" Moving a king-size sofa bed is a major undertaking. Its weight makes it difficult to lift. Its bulkiness might prevent it from fitting through some doorways. A large china closet is heavy, bulky, and fragile as well. It too is a difficult item to move.

Another question to ask when considering a piece of furniture might be: "Could I use this in a different climate or in a different style of home?"

A third consideration is: "How adaptable will this piece of furniture be?" It is a good idea to choose furniture that can function as well and look as good in a living room as in a bedroom. The nightstand in your bedroom may have to serve as an end table in the living room of your next apartment. Or it could be used as the telephone table in the hall of your first house.

Reduced Housekeeping Time. Today, fewer people than ever before are able or willing to devote many hours a week to the chores of housework. Certainly, many women who once stayed at home full-time now choose to work outside the home. But that is not the only reason that less housework is done. Many families, nowadays, are headed by a single breadwinner. Even if someone has many hours available for housekeeping, that person often chooses to spend time doing things that are rewarding.

How does this change in life-style affect the interior-design choices? It means that ease of maintenance may be a priority. You might like the look of fragile, light-color upholstery. But you would probably choose a sturdier fabric treated with stain-repellent instead. Or, you might opt for a light-color leatherette upholstery that can be wiped clean.

Smaller Living Spaces. Today, we tend to live in rooms, apartments, and houses that are smaller than the ones people lived in years ago. For one thing, building costs have risen to the point where many people cannot find or afford spacious living accommodations. For another thing, we have become extremely fuel-conscious. Thus we are unwilling to commit ourselves to the waste or cost involved in heating large homes. A third consideration is property taxes, which have been steadily on the rise. Smaller homes mean lower taxes.

What are the interior design problems that result from this life-style change? There are several. One is that the individual pieces of furniture must be kept relatively small in size if they are to look at home in small rooms. Another is that we must limit the amount of furniture we acquire. A third is that we must sometimes select furniture that can be used in more than one way.

Fewer Storage Areas. New buildings include fewer closets, cupboards, pantries, and shelves than older buildings. In new houses, attics and basements may be smaller or eliminated altogether. To save costs, builders have been eliminating these built-in storage spaces. They have also been using one larger room to take the place of several smaller ones. For instance, a single open space may fill the need for a living room, dining room, and family room. These changes affect interior design. In buying furnishings, you might choose some furniture that can be used to separate and define different use areas as well as provide space for needed storage. For example, a tall bookcase-and-cupboard unit can separate the dining area from the living area. At the same time, it will provide a place for dishes, placemats, napkins, silverware, and the like. If a house is short of closet space, a low trunk might be a better choice of furniture than a coffee table. The trunk could do everything a coffee table does and at the same time provide storage space for out-of-season clothes.

Changing Patterns of Entertainment. Our life-style has also changed over the years in the way in which we entertain friends in the home. Gone are the formal

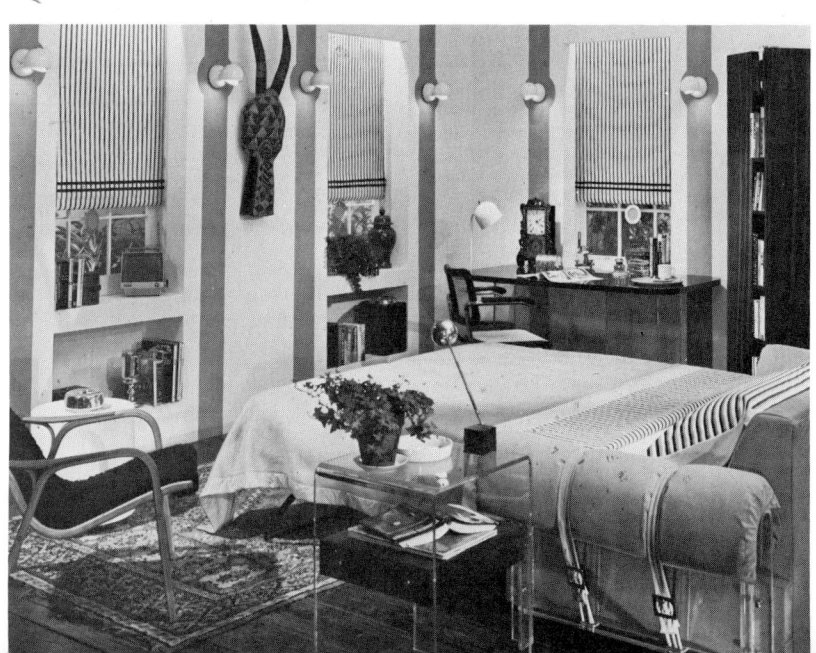

This handsome room has multiple uses, a contemporary design feature which reflects the trend toward smaller housing.

dinners for twelve or twenty people. Gone are the elaborate luncheons that took days to prepare. As a rule, we tend to entertain more casually. We also tend to invite smaller groups of people. We should recognize this life-style change when we furnish our homes. The furniture we select, the way in which we arrange it, and the tableware can be chosen to reflect the way we enjoy ourselves best with friends.

THE PSYCHOLOGICAL BENEFITS OF INTERIOR DESIGN

Becoming skilled in the art and craft of effective interior design has yet another benefit to offer you. It can make you feel good.

Psychologists say that the home in which you live has an important bearing on your sense of well-being. A room that you find comfortable and attractive and that is arranged to meet your life-style makes you feel good about yourself and about life in general. In the same way, a room that you don't like—even if you are not sure why—can make you feel dissatisfied and irritable.

Another psychological truth is that everyone enjoys feeling some ability to control the environment. Making choices gives people a sense of power. They feel that they are, to some extent, controlling their own world. Choosing how to furnish a living space can be an exercise in asserting your identity and control within your environment. You may not be able to remake the whole world to your liking. But through interior design, you can at least remake your corner. And that's a very good thing.

A third possible psychological benefit that can come from effective interior design is receiving the approval of others. The successful interior design meets not only your needs but also the needs of other people who use that space. Your home can be pleasant, attractive, and comfortable to family, friends, and visitors. Their comfort, pleasure, and approval will help you to feel good about yourself.

THE LIFETIME VALUES OF INTERIOR-DESIGN SKILLS

For as long as you live, you will be housed in a room, an apartment, or a dwelling of some sort. How you furnish these homes will always be important to your happiness and your personal growth.

Long-Term Needs. No matter where you live, there will be some furnishings that you will take with you from place to place. These furnishings will meet a permanent need in your life. Thus, you will want to choose them for their permanent qualities of comfort and beauty. Over the years, they will come to have increasing emotional importance to you.

You will probably acquire these furnishings one at a time over a long period of time. Some may be antiques for which you will enjoy searching. Some may represent a geographical area where you spent especially happy times. A striking painting, a handmade rug, a handsome chest of drawers, or a lovely piece of pottery—all your finds will become part of the growing collection of things you

Home furnishings can establish a sense of continuity in personal and family life. Learning to remodel and refinish old furniture can be economically and emotionally rewarding. Can you think of any furniture that needs restoring in your home?

cherish. These treasures will make you feel at home the moment you unpack them. So recognizing permanent qualities of beauty and usefulness is a skill you will always need and use.

Short-Term Needs. But you will also have a continuing need to select furnishings on a short-term basis, to fill immediate needs. You may choose to leave these furnishings behind when you make your next move or when your interests change. Or you may develop useful skills in learning to remodel, refinish, or even remake this sort of furniture to meet your changing needs. The ability to see what can be changed effectively or put to a new and different use will be of constant value to you.

Energy Tips

A decision or commitment to be energy-conscious becomes part of one's lifestyle. Our habits give us away: Do we use the dryer for one shirt, or do we hang the shirt to dry; leave the television on when no one is watching, or turn it off; leave an air conditioner on when no one is home, or turn it on only when needed?

Some people choose to buy many electric appliances for kitchen use; others keep appliances to a minimum or use hand-operated ones. People who make an effort to conserve energy show an aware, concerned, and positive attitude. Uninformed people give the impression of wastefulness and lack of concern.

Even if you do not move, there may be many reasons for you to rearrange your furniture over the years. So it will help you to acquire an understanding of the principles behind successful furniture arrangement.

The Need For Change. Periodically, there will be the need to change your furnishings simply from a need for change. If the room that is your bedroom now were to remain your bedroom all the days of your life, you would certainly want to re-do it now and then, simply to break the monotony. A working knowledge and understanding of the basics of interior design is something that you will find useful throughout your life.

This book is designed to introduce you to the skills and understandings you will need to make sure that every apartment or house you ever live in is as attractive, comfortable, and efficient as it can be. It will help you to give your home the special mark, or signature, of the unique person who was its designer: you.

Careers

An interior designer plans and furnishes interiors of houses, offices, hotels, clubs, and studios. The designer meets the needs of a variety of people and is an expert on home furnishings. This career demands an interest in people, flexibility with a variety of tastes, good business sense, and a pleasant personality. It is a creative and competitive field requiring overtime and irregular hours. The pay is high.

A license is required after training in an accredited institute. Necessary courses include art history, color, mechanical drawing, business fundamentals, home furnishings, and building construction. You can acquire practical experience by arranging sets for school plays or working part-time in a furniture showroom.

Learning Experiences

1. From a magazine featuring photographs of room designs, choose a picture of a room that you find attractive and suitable for your own personality and life-style. In your report, explain why the room design would be a good one for you. Also include your thoughts about the person or family who might find it to be an inappropriate choice.
2. Prepare a short report telling which of your own needs, which needs of other members of your family, and which needs of your friends you would consider in redesigning your own room at home. What compromises would have to be made?
3. What does *taste* mean? How would you describe your own taste in home furnishings? Make a list of people, experiences, stores, homes, and other influences that you think have had an important role in developing your own taste.
4. Devise a simple but logical system for filing, storing, and relocating clippings, photographs, fabric samples, and other resources you will accumulate as an "idea file" for your future interior-design projects.
5. Create a dual-purpose room. Use magazine illustrations to describe a room which could serve two functions. Evaluate your room for advantages and disadvantages.
6. Choose one interior-design project which your family could work on together. Choose a project that would allow your family to enjoy both the effort and the results. How much would it cost? How would you organize the procedure and how could you arouse family interest in it?

CHAPTER 2

Color! Color! Color!

Have you ever noticed the way a baby will reach out for a brightly colored object? That is a natural response. All of us react to color. As children, we tend to like bright, clear colors best. As we grow older, our taste in colors may change. We begin to appreciate more subtle colors and color combinations.

Color affects our reaction to almost everything. Because everyone does respond to color, the use of it is of basic importance in interior design.

Personal Taste. It is important to keep in mind, however, that color preferences are a matter of personal taste. Some people, for example, like rooms decorated in such dark colors as navy blue, chocolate brown, and charcoal gray. People who like those colors describe such rooms as being "snug and warm" or "cozy and comfortable." Other people do not like dark colors in the rooms. To them, dark colors are "depressing" or "gloomy." Similarly, some people find rooms decorated in bright, strong colors "cheerful" and "lively." But others may find that such rooms make them feel nervous or jumpy.

Color Use. The way in which a person responds to a color also depends upon the way that color is used. For example, few people would choose black as their

---

Energy Tips

Colors or hues can sometimes enhance the work of the energy source. Interior designers may use reds, pinks, and oranges to warm a room that always feels cold, such as one with northern exposure. Blues and greens psychologically give a cool feeling and are especially useful in rooms with inadequate air circulation or in rooms near heat sources.

favorite color. Many might even say, "I hate the color black!" Yet those same people see the beauty of black trees outlined against a pale gray sky and a field of new-fallen snow. And they might be the first to choose an all-black lamp to give a bit of "zip" to a room they were furnishing. White is also seldom chosen as a favorite color. Yet, most of us respond positively to an all-white summer dress. We also like white walls that serve as a background for brightly colored paintings. And many people choose to hang white curtains at a window. There will probably be a place in your design world for every color imaginable, depending upon how and where you choose to use it.

Color Associations. The way we respond to certain combinations of colors has less to do with the colors themselves than with the associations they bring to mind. For example, imagine a room decorated in a color scheme of red, white, and blue. What would that make you think of? In the United States, it is almost impossible for people to see red, white, and blue without thinking of the flag.

All of these general observations lead to one conclusion: Your choice of colors in any interior design should not be made only on the basis of which colors you love. The world of color is a complicated one. You need to know facts about color before you can hope to use it successfully.

BASIC FACTS ABOUT COLOR

The subject of color is so complex that many whole books have been devoted to it. In this book, however, it is necessary only to deal with color as it applies to the home. We will be concerned with the colors of paints, stains, dyes, and fabrics. But before we can consider how color is used, we need to know what color is.

Color is a basic element in interior design. A knowledge of what color is and an understanding of the different qualities in colors, such as hue, value, and intensity, can be very helpful in selecting a pleasing color scheme.

Basic Colors

Have you ever looked at "color chips" in a paint store—those little cards showing samples of different shades of paint? You may think that the colors on the cards are created by mixing many different colors. The fact is, however, that all these shades can be made by mixing only three basic colors.

Primary Colors. There are three colors with which all designers must begin: red, yellow, and blue. These colors are called *primary colors* because they cannot be created by mixing other colors.

Primitive people produced primary colors in several ways. They could make colors by crushing stones or by drying and crushing clays. Or they could crush shells or squeeze the fluid from the petals of flowers. Today, we can buy red, yellow, and blue coloring matter in paints, in dyes, or in dry, powdery pigments. Using these three colors, we can mix any color in the world, including blacks, tans, browns, and grays.

To simplify our study of color, we have spaced the three primary colors at equal intervals on a circle. We have also arranged them in the same relationship you see in a natural rainbow in the sky, or in a rainbow you create by holding a prism in the sunlight.

Secondary Colors. When you mix equal amounts of any two of the three primary colors, you create an entirely new color. Equal amounts of red and yellow produce orange. Equal amounts of yellow and blue produce green. Equal amounts of blue and red produce violet. The new colors can then be placed halfway between the two primary colors used to produce them. Colors produced by mixing two primary colors are called *secondary colors*. Orange, green, and violet are secondary colors.

Intermediate Colors. If you mix equal amounts of one secondary color and one primary color, you will produce yet another set of colors. These new colors can be placed halfway between the secondary and the primary colors that were used to create them. Colors created by mixing one primary and one secondary color are called *intermediate colors*. Thus, by mixing colors and placing the new colors on the circle, you gradually create a color wheel. In this way, you can reproduce with paint the colors that light produces in the rainbow and that you find in paint chips.

Neutral Colors. When all three primary colors are mixed together, it is possible to create tans, browns, grays, and blacks—the colors which are called *neutrals*. These neutral colors can also be created by mixing the three secondary colors. If you think about how the secondary colors were themselves created, you will understand why mixing the three secondary colors together will give the same result as mixing the three primary colors together.

Neutralized Colors. Colors can be softened, or grayed, in one of two ways. You can mix some of the neutral colors into the colors on the circle. Or you can mix into one of the colors on the circle any primary color that was not used in its creation. For example, suppose you want to soften the color green. One way to do it would be to mix into it a little black, which is a neutral color. Another way to do it would be to mix a little bit of red, because red is the primary color that is not used in making the green itself. Blue, in which there is not yellow or red, can be grayed by mixing a little black into it—or by mixing into it the remaining two primaries. When a color has been softened this way, it is called a *neutralized color*.

Basic Color Qualities

Every color in the world has three qualities: hue, value, and intensity. By describing these qualities, we can help others to imagine the particular color we have in mind. By analyzing these qualities, we can understand how to use color effectively.

Hue. The name of a color usually indicates its hue. In fact, the word *color,* as it is commonly used, is synonymous with *hue*. The hue name, however, is often the more basic and accurate term. For example, the hue blue might be given the color name *azure* or *sky-blue*. The hue of a fire might be yellow, red-orange, or orange, but its color name might be *flame*. Commercial color names can be even more imaginative. *Luggage tan, shocking pink,* and *poison green* are typical. They are suggestive names, but they are not really precise.

When two hue names are used to describe a single color, the second of the two names is the dominant color. For example, *yellow-green* names a color that is green but that has more yellow than blue in it. *Greenish-yellow,* on the other hand, is a color that is yellow but with some green in it.

Value. The value of a color is that quality which you see in a black and white photograph. You know that the object photographed has color. You also know that what you are seeing in the photograph is simply the color's relative lightness or darkness. A color's lightness or darkness is its *value*. If the value is light, it is called a *tint* of a color (as pink is a tint of red). If the value is dark, it is called a *shade* of a color (as maroon is a shade of red). If the value of a color is about halfway between a tint and a shade, it is called a *middle value*.

Value is a very important concept to understand in dealing with colors in home furnishings. The value of a color can affect how large an object looks. Have you ever noticed that dark clouds in a light sky seem to be closer and, therefore, larger than light clouds of the same size that blend with the light sky? In the same way, a dark sofa in a light room will seem to be larger than it really it. But if the room has dark walls, the dark sofa will blend into the dark walls and seem to be smaller. A strong contrast of values will emphasize the size of objects. But similar values will reduce the apparent size of an object.

Intensity. The brightness or dullness, strength or weakness of a color is its *intensity*. At first, you may think that intensity is the same as value, but they are different. Intense colors are clear and bright. Less-intense colors are grayed or dull. Highly intense colors spring out at you, while colors of low intensity fade into the background.

223

This kitchen-dining area uses neutral color as a background for small, colorful furnishings. Notice how the small decorative tin seems to stand out.

In nature, the smaller the object, the more brilliant or intense the color will usually be. The larger the object, the duller and grayer the color will be. For example, flowers, butterflies, and small fish are usually brilliant or intense in color. But forests, elephants, and whales are dull in color.

In using color in home furnishings, a safe policy is to follow this rule of nature: Use the intense colors on the small objects in a room, such as pillows, area rugs, small chairs, and accessories. Use the softer, duller colors on the walls, the floors, the sofas, and the large chairs.

This is not to say that you *must* follow this rule of nature. Skilled decorators can use large expanses of bright color for exciting, dramatic effects. But going against a rule of nature can be very tricky. Unless you're sure of what you're doing, you might find yourself overwhelmed by color.

Two Basic Divisions of Hues

All hues can be divided into two general categories: warm and cool. A hue will be either warm or cool by itself or by contrast to other hues.

Warm Hues. Hues which have either a yellow or a red dominance are warm hues. Think of the sun. Think of fire. Warm hues are exciting and stimulating.

Energy Tips

Wise use of light and dark colors can save on energy costs. Less electric lighting is necessary in a room with light colors and reflective wall surfaces. Ceilings painted with light colors will reflect light back into the room. Dark colors absorb light. A black house with a black roof will have added warmth in the winter but may require extra cooling in the summer.

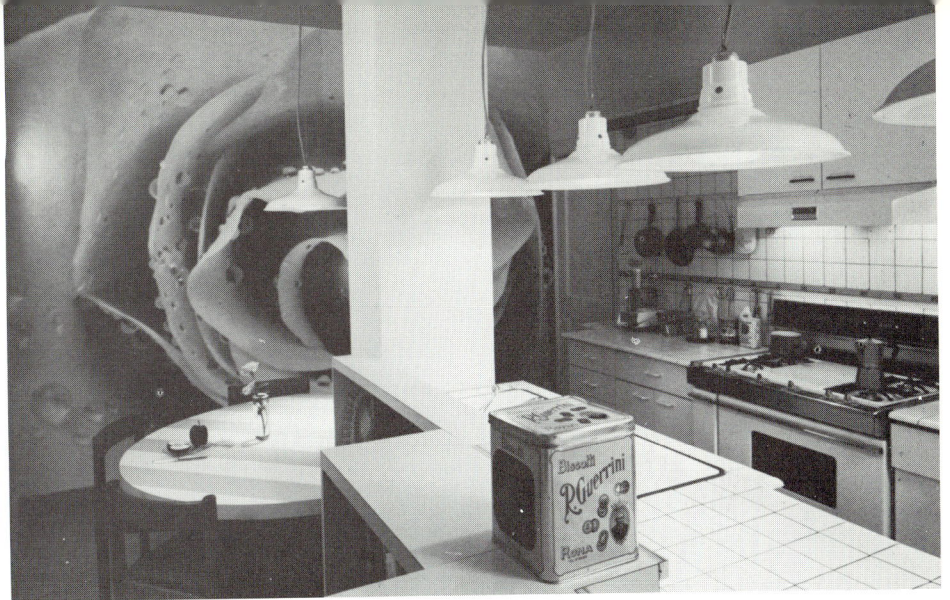

The addition of a colorful and dramatic wall painting changes the focus in the kitchen. Does the small tin seem so prominent now?

They seem to come forward and demand your attention wherever they are used. Look at the rows of people the next time you are in a large auditorium or sports arena. Notice how any clothes that are red, orange, or yellow seem to jump out of the crowd and catch your eye. Because of this "advancing" quality, anything in a warm color will seem larger or more prominent than it really is. Walls done in a strong, warm color will advance and make the room seem smaller than it is.

Cool Hues. Hues which have a dominance of blue are cool hues. Think of water, sky, ice, and snow. Cool hues are quieting and soothing. They seem to recede into the distance. For that reason, cool-colored objects will appear to recede if the color is not too intense. They will seem to be smaller than they really are. Walls of a light, cool color will also appear to recede. Such walls will make a room seem larger than it is.

There are two hues that are evenly balanced in warmth and coolness. They are made up of equal parts of warm and cool color. They are green (made up of blue, which is cool, and yellow, which is warm) and violet (made up of red, which is warm, and blue, which is cool). If either of these colors, green or violet, is used with a warm color, it will look cool by comparison. If either is used with a cool color, it will look warm. Thus, green can "cool down" a color scheme of yellow and orange. It can also "warm up" a color scheme of blue shades and tints. The same is true of violet.

Basic Effects of Colors on Each Other

In selecting colors for the furnishings of a room, think of them all as a part of a group rather than as separate colors. Every color in any grouping will affect all the other colors in that group, just as each individual at a party affects everybody else there. For example, a life-of-the-party type can silence everybody else and make them seem dull by comparison. But if the life-of-the-party type

The color interest in this room is intensified by the complexity of light, textures, and patterns. What feelings are conveyed by this design?

leaves, the rest of the people in the room suddenly have a chance to talk and seem more interesting and alive. In the same way, an intense color can make all the other, softer colors in a room look dull. Remove that intense color and the remaining colors can emerge with a beauty of their own.

Hue Changes.   Like people, colors seem different in different settings. This is especially true if the color is a quiet, subtle one. Have you ever noticed that a certain item of clothing seems to change color depending on what other colors are near it? If you wear a blue-green shirt with green pants and a green jacket, the shirt is likely to look distinctly blue by contrast. Change to blue pants and a blue jacket, and the color of the shirt seems to change to green. Because of this tendency of colors to "change" hue, depending upon what other colors they are near, it's a good idea to hold samples of colors next to each other before you make your final selection for use in a room design. That way, you can be certain that the hues you pick will end up looking the way you want them to look when they are combined with other hues.

Value Changes.   Another startling change produced in a color results from the values of the other colors it is placed near. A light-colored shirt will make a dark-skinned person look darker. A dark-colored shirt will make the same person look lighter. In the same way, a wall that is light will make a carpet that is middle value look darker than it is. That same carpet in a dark, wood-paneled room will look almost light by comparison.

Intensity Changes.   The larger the area a color occupies, the more intense it will seem. A single sprig of forsythia, for example, seems fairly pale in color. But a whole forsythia bush in bloom appears to be a bright, intense yellow. By the same token, you may choose a rug or wallpaper based on a small sample in a showroom. But when yards and yards of that carpeting or wallpaper are actually installed in a room, you may find that the great quantity of the color has made it seem darker and more intense. The solution to this problem is to choose colors slightly lighter and duller than you really want for use in large areas. Then, when they are used in large quantities, the colors will appear more intense and darker—the colors you wanted originally.

Effect of Light, Texture, and Pattern on Color

So far, we have been discussing color simply as color. But colors come into our homes as a part of something else. They never stand alone. In considering color as it is applied to home furnishings, we must take account of three additional elements that affect it.

Light. Color is affected by light, not only the amount of light that shines upon it but the kind of light as well. Suppose you plan to cover a chair in blue fabric, and you have chosen the shade of blue you prefer. How that color will actually look once it is on the chair in your room will depend on where the chair is to stand. The blue may have one appearance near a window in bright sunlight. It may look quite different in the same position on a dull day or after dark. The color will also change depending upon the kind of light that falls on it. Natural sunlight, incandescent light (the kind that comes from regular electric light bulbs), and fluorescent light (the kind that comes from long, tubular electric-light fixtures) will each have a different effect upon the color of your chair. For this reason, whenever possible, it is a good idea to bring home a sample of any fabric, carpet, or wallpaper you are considering. Place it in the room where you hope to use it. That way, you can see what changes (if any) take place under the particular light conditions of the room.

Texture. Texture refers to the relative roughness or smoothness of an object. The smoother something is, the less texture it is said to have. Glass, chrome, and highly polished woods have almost no texture at all. Burlap, rough-cast plaster, and unglazed tile have a great deal of surface texture.

Texture affects color. A rough surface will cast small, almost invisible shadows that soften or "break up" the color that is applied to it. In the case of a wall covered with a solid-color wallpaper, the lack of texture on the paper surface will make bright colors unbearably strong and gaudy. A clear, light yellow would probably be a poor choice for an untextured wall. But the same color used on a rough-textured plaster or papered wall could be very appealing. In the same way, a clear yellow dye used on a coarse fabric might be quite beautiful. The same dye used on a smooth-surfaced fabric (such as satin) might be too harsh and glaring to be attractive. As a general rule, clear, bright colors look less harsh on surfaces that have some degree of texture than they do on smooth surfaces.

Pattern. When paper or fabric is not a solid color but carries a design on it, we say that it is patterned. There are many different kinds of patterns in all sizes and color combinations. Some patterns have a very formal, elegant appearance.

Others are breezy and casual. Almost every room design will benefit if there is some use of pattern in it.

It is important to remember that each pattern has its own beauty and each needs to be separated from all other patterns by a plain or textured surface. That way, individual patterns can be shown off to their best advantage.

Some of the many types of patterns you will find are these:

Realistic. These patterns feature recognizable objects in their designs. People, animals, buildings, birds, flowers—anything that is found in the world may end up as the subject of a figurative pattern. These patterns may be highly realistic, duplicating objects with almost photographic exactness. Or they may be very impressionistic, as when only a few brush strokes form a flower's petals. Floral patterns are, perhaps, the most popular of all realistic designs.

Conventionalized. This type of pattern starts with a realistic or recognizable object. The designer then simplifies the object and changes it to produce a pleasing design that can be enjoyed from every direction. This type of pattern, because it has no "up" or "down," makes an excellent choice for carpets and upholstery fabrics.

Abstract. These patterns are frequently based on the forms of geometry. Forms such as the circle, square, triangle, straight line, and so on are presented in a precise, mathematical order. They are extremely regular in their appearance. When used on large areas, they are very demanding and lead the eye in straight lines—vertically, horizontally, or diagonally. Abstract patterns occur in nature, as on dried clay, crystals, seashells, and tortoise shells. In looking at such a pattern, you can't see where the design stops and starts.

A color will be affected by any other colors appearing in the same pattern with it. In the same way, a pattern is affected by any other pattern that is near it. Combining two different patterns, side by side, can be especially tricky. For this reason, many designers use patterns sparingly. In addition, they usually separate any patterns they are using from one another by stretches of solid color.

CHOOSING A COLOR COMBINATION

The choosing of colors to combine into a color scheme is the first step toward using them in a room. As you may have guessed from the discussion of color, this is not as easy to do well as you might once have thought. Fortunately, creating a color scheme can be simplified in any of several ways.

Sources of Color Schemes. The best source of timelessly beautiful color combinations is nature. Think of the color schemes found in different types of landscapes—the jungle, the forest, the ocean shore, the rolling countryside. The desert, which some people don't regard as colorful, has inspired beautiful room designs. In such rooms, the colors of clay, rock, and sand are used in subtle combinations of pattern and texture.

The realistic pattern of this dining area's wallpaper employs flowers. Notice also the contrast of the striped paper in the kitchen.

Flowers have been conventionalized into a pattern in this wallpaper. Natural-wood floors and exposed-beam ceiling of this country-style dining area add to an informal warmth and hospitality.

A large-scale, geometrically designed wallpaper pattern is very demanding to the eye. Here the background wall establishes the formal tone of the dining room.

Next, consider the insects, butterflies, fish, birds, and other animals. Many of them offer exciting and unusual color-combination ideas.

Consider the flowers, the shells, the rocks. These items from nature offer infinite color combinations. Any one of them can provide you with a color scheme of timeless beauty.

Another rich possibility to explore in your search for a color scheme is the work of great artists. Museums and galleries are filled with masterpieces that can suggest color combinations. You could also consider a variety of handmade and machine-manufactured objects made by artist crafts workers. Oriental or Indian rugs, fine porcelain dinnerware, exotic fabrics are just a few of the items you can study in your search for a color combination.

All of this color awareness develops your own taste and color sense. The only unbreakable rule in choosing a color scheme for an interior design is that it must be a combination of colors that appeals to you.

Limits on Choices. What if you don't have complete freedom to choose what you want? What if you are designing a room where one of the colors is already determined? Suppose there is wall-to-wall carpeting on the floor, and you cannot replace it. Or suppose that you live in a rented apartment where only the landlord is allowed to choose colors for the walls. When you are "locked in" to using one or more colors, you need to look for a color combination that will include that color. While that limits your choices, it need not prevent you from coming up with an enjoyable, successful design—even if the color you must use is one you don't especially like. By choosing carefully and designing around the color you are stuck with, you can either make that color seem less important or even turn it into a real advantage. It takes time, effort, and imagination to do this. But you can do it if you want to.

IDENTIFYING AND USING COLOR SCHEMES

A color scheme is a combination of two or more colors used together according to a plan. It is a plan that follows definite principles. It is used to choose colors and to determine how those colors will relate to each other. The relationship of the colors you have chosen to the other colors on the color wheel will determine the kind of color scheme you have devised.

Related Color Schemes

Related color schemes are those which use a small section of the color wheel at most. All the colors in a related color scheme lie close together on the color wheel. There are two main types of related color schemes.

Monochromatic Color Schemes. Generally, a monochromatic scheme includes various values and variations of a single hue combined with a single neutral color. Alternatively, such a scheme may use several neutrals or shades of a neutral, with just a single strong color as an accent. A view of the ocean—blue water, blue sky, and whitecaps—would be a typical example of a monochromatic color scheme in which several shades of a single hue (blue) were combined with a single neutral (white). A blue jay, on the other hand, is an example of a monochromatic scheme in which a single hue (blue) is combined with several neutrals (white, gray, black). Also, a neutral can become the important, or dominant, factor, and the color, the accent. Think of the swan. White, which is neutral, is the important color. A splash of orange (the beak) provides the accent.

When used in a room, any of these variations on the monochromatic scheme produces a feeling of complete unity.

Analogous Color Schemes. The second type of related color scheme begins with a dominant color and a neutral (or a group of neutrals). It then adds one or two other colors that are close to the dominant one on the color wheel. Thus, a combination of blue, blue-green, and green would make an analogous color scheme. A neutral, such as white, could be added to the combination.

When an analogous scheme is used in a room, one of the colors or neutrals should be clearly dominant, or most important. As with the monochromatic scheme, rooms decorated with an analogous color scheme create a strong sense of unity. But they have the added drama of a slightly wider range of color.

Contrasting Color Schemes

Contrasting color schemes are made up of colors that represent the entire color wheel. Because of the wider range of colors included, contrasting color schemes are especially effective in large rooms. Still, it is necessary to create a sense of unity in these schemes. The simplest way to do this is to select and use the dominant hue, softened and grayed, over a large enough area to be strongly established. The other hue or hues and the neutrals in the scheme can then be used in smaller areas as accents.

Complementary Color Schemes. Colors directly opposite one another on the color wheel are called *complementary colors*. A color scheme based on two such colors is called a complementary color scheme. Suppose that you are attracted by the colors of a cherry tree, with its bright red fruit and green leaves. You will find that these colors are opposite one another on the color wheel. Thus, a room based on a combination of red and green would have a complementary color scheme.

Because the use of two complementary colors is always very dramatic, it is especially important to lower the intensity of one of the dominant colors and to add a generous use of one or more of the neutrals. In nature, the green of the cherry-tree leaves is dominant, the red of the cherries is the accent, and the brown of the tree bark is the neutral. A room done entirely in red and green would seem overpowering to most people. A free use of browns, tans, off-white, and a neutralized green would tame the color scheme without robbing it of its drama.

Split Complementary Color Schemes. This type of color scheme is a three-color harmony. First, find a color of your choice on the color wheel. (Suppose you have chosen red.) Next, find its complementary color—green. Then find the two hues that lie on either side of the complementary color. (The colors on the wheel on

Not all wallpapers use a repeating pattern. Random-match papers can create a varying design that establishes a light, informal mood.

either side of green are yellow-green and blue-green.) These three colors, red, yellow-green, and blue-green, together form a split complementary color scheme. Of course, you would probably want to add one or more neutrals to this type of scheme. Either the neutral or one of the three hues could be the dominant color in the scheme, with the others serving as accent colors.

Triadic Color Schemes. A triadic color scheme is a three-color harmony in which the colors are equal distances from one another on the color wheel. If you start with red, you would use yellow and blue as the second and third colors in your scheme. If you begin with green, violet and orange would be the second and third colors. Because triadic schemes tend to be very dramatic, they also benefit from the free use of neutrals to tame them down.

USING COLOR IN A ROOM

You have chosen the basic colors you wish to work with. You have refined your choice by converting it into a specific color scheme. Now you must begin to plan the effective use of your color scheme in a room.

A beautiful color scheme can make any room lovely, regardless of how unattractive or inexpensive the furnishings are. Well used, color is like a magic wand that can turn a dreary, dull room into a beautiful place to live.

Unfortunately, the reverse is also true. Color can be used so poorly that it can ruin a room in which many individually beautiful furnishings have been placed. For this reason, the next section on how to *use* color schemes is most important.

Adapting Color Schemes to Rooms

The safest and most certain way to produce beauty with a color scheme is to follow the patterns found in nature. Learn the principles of how color is used in nature. Then adapt these principles to the interior of your home. In that way, you are certain to end up with a room design in which color is used well.

Choosing a Dominant Color. The first step in putting color into a room is to choose one color to be dominant. *Dominant* means most important. As a rule of thumb, the dominant color should be used on 60 percent of the large areas of the room, including floors, walls, ceiling, and large pieces of furniture.

In nature, one constant color principle is: the larger an area, the grayer the color. The smaller the area, the brighter the color. Adapting this principle to your choice of a dominant color, you would select either a neutral or a hue which has been grayed, or softened. Even the grayed colors found in nature have infinite small variations that give them textural beauty and depth. The fact that your dominant color is neutral need not mean that it must be dull. Neutrals can have many small variations. Receding ocean waves leave a constantly changing pattern of darker tan on the light tan of the dry sand on the shore. In the desert, the wind produces ripples on the sand that cast patterns of shadows. And the wind affects the snow in the same way, producing an equally beautiful textured pattern of shadows in gray or soft blue, depending on the light.

Choosing Accent Colors. The remaining colors in your color scheme will automatically be the accent colors. But these need not all be used in equal amounts. If you have more than one accent color in your scheme, plan which of them will be the most important accent, which will be the second most important accent, and so on.

Planning the Color Placement. After the colors are chosen, you need to begin thinking about where they will be used. Since the neutralized dominant color will be covering nearly two-thirds of the room and furnishings, begin by deciding on its placement. The simplest way is to use the dominant color on two of the three large room surfaces: floor, walls, ceiling. If the room has large windows, the curtains that cover them would be another major area. Any large piece of furniture, such as a sofa or bed, would be yet another place to use the dominant color.

Another step in planning color in a room is to see that color is used at different levels. A rug, of course, is at floor level. Seating-upholstery and

Gradation in color from light to dark is another element to be considered in any design scheme.

bedspreads would bring the color a third of the way up from the floor. Curtains and decorative objects on the wall help move the color still higher.

Suppose you are designing a living room in a green, gold, and blue color scheme. Green could be the dominant color in your scheme. If you used a soft green rug, green draw-curtains over a large picture window, and a green, tweedy sofa, you would have covered about 60 percent of the room with the dominant color. Also, you would have used it at varying heights. Off-white could be used on walls and ceiling as a background color. Gold, green, and blue could appear in upholstery, lamps, and small objects to introduce accents.

Tan walls, a tan print bedspread, and tan wooden shutters would effectively establish the dominant color in a monochromatic bedroom in which tan was to be dominant. A tweed rug of tan, off-white, and chocolate brown could be used. Orange bed pillows would introduce the accent color.

Choosing a Scheme of Values. The use of dark or light values in colors or neutrals has an important effect on a room. Here, again, nature is an excellent guide. Notice that darkness makes the world close in around you, while lightness expands the world to the horizon. The same holds true in room design. Dark walls and dark ceilings tend to make the room feel enclosed. Light walls and light ceilings create the opposite effect, a sense of space and freedom. Which effect do you want to establish in your room?

Another pattern that nature usually follows is the use of color values on the ground that are darker than the values of objects at eye level. Things high overhead—sky, clouds, sun—are lighter still. Putting this principle into practice in room planning would lead you to choose a medium-dark floor covering, wall colors of middle values, and a ceiling of light value. On the other hand, just as a dark, stormy sky can be very dramatic, so can a ceiling be dramatic if it is darker in value than the walls and floor. Keep in mind, however, that not everyone is comfortable in dramatic situations for long periods of time. Also, remember that the dark value of the ceiling will make it seem lower than it really is.

Another value tip from nature is this. On bright days, people tend to feel very peppy and active. On gray days, they tend to feel more subdued and quiet. On really dark days, they tend to go to sleep. Choose the mood you want to produce in your room. Then select the colors you have chosen in the values that will produce that mood.

For example, light walls and ceiling, middle values for floor and upholstery, and sparkling accent colors will make a room look big and sunny and will make it feel alive. A dark ceiling with light walls and with dark and light floor and upholstery will be exciting and dramatic, like a stormy scene. Dark wood-paneled walls with a light ceiling and a middle value on the floor will seem cozy and snug, and seem like a small clearing in the woods.

But before you make a firm decision about color values, analyze the climate in which you live. Remember, too, that you will be using your room the whole year round. If the climate is hot for substantial parts of the year, you will want to choose a scheme that will make your room seem cool and airy. If the climate is cold, you may prefer to try for an effect of warmth and coziness.

Using Color in Patterns and Textures

Since color does not stand on its own, we must take another step once the color scheme is chosen and the placement of the colors determined. We must decide what the personality of the room is to be. We must also determine whether the surfaces will be plain, patterned, textured, or smooth. These choices will have a direct effect on the personality or mood of a room.

Large Patterns. Large patterns have a tendency to make a room seem very dramatic and sophisticated. They should be used sparingly because they will make a room seem smaller than it is. Also, it is generally a good practice not to combine a large pattern with any other patterns. The other patterns will make it less dramatic. If you choose a large pattern for any area of your room (walls, floor covering, upholstery, or other fabric design) the remaining areas should be treated with solid color.

Small Patterns. Small patterns are far easier to handle than large ones. They can also be used in greater quantity. Small patterns tend to make a room look informal and cozy. However, too much of a small pattern will make the room look fussy and cluttered.

Textures. Textures, like patterns, have their own unique role to play in the appearance of a room. Smooth walls, rugs, and fabrics have a tendency to look elegant and dignified. Think of silk, satin, polished steel, chrome, and glass. The smoother the textures are, the sleeker they are. And sleekness suggests elegance. Rough textures, on the other hand, suggest informality, warmth, and coziness.

There is no reason, of course, why you cannot use some slightly rough textures and some smooth textures in the same room. The combination can lend interest and variety to a room design. Some fabrics, such as leather and vinyl, can be used effectively in rooms that are primarily either smooth-textured or rough-textured.

The dramatic strength of this large-patterned area rug is a colorful addition to the otherwise neutral color scheme.

General Principles. To help you in making your selections and combinations, however, keep these general principles in mind. Keep patterns separated from each other by areas of solid color. For instance, suppose you have chosen a patterned fabric for draperies. But you have a fabric in a different pattern for some of the upholstered furniture. It can be disastrous to place a piece of furniture with patterned upholstery in front of the differently patterned draperies. Use a piece of furniture upholstered in a solid color in front of the draperies. Then place the patterned furniture against a solid-colored wall. By the same token, a patterned rug will be safe to use in a room with plain walls, plain draperies, and furniture upholstered in a solid color. Pictures show up best on a plain wall. So if your walls are patterned, be sure that any pictures are framed with large, solid-color mats. These mats will separate the picture area from the surrounding wall pattern.

Making Decisions About Color. Trial and error is probably a good way to help you decide about color in a room design. Get small swatches of different colors, fabrics, or wallpapers. Try moving these samples around and lining them up in different combinations. Which do you prefer? Can you tell why? Which do you dislike? Can you tell why?

Designing a room is a major undertaking. Don't settle for the first possible combination, or the second, or even the tenth or twelfth. You want to be sure that it is a combination of colors and patterns and textures that you like. Be sure, too, that it is a choice you can live with happily for a long time to come. You will find that your skill and your judgment will improve as you study and experiment.

Careers

Opportunities exist for a career in photographing furniture displays for magazines, books, and newspapers. If you have hobbies which include art, photography, drawing designs, or helping people arrange their furnishings, you might become part of this glamorous profession.

There are many entry-level jobs. Some of these are magazine production assistant, photographer's assistant, department-store salesperson in the furniture-accessories department, textile salesperson, and store-display designer or arranger. The requirements for this career are a thorough knowledge of photography, an artistic awareness, and initiative. A college degree in art may be useful but is not required.

Some of the duties of the photographer include creating the furniture layout and displays; choosing color schemes with matching accessories and backgrounds; keeping up with new products and market trends; working with stores, magazines, and photographic suppliers; and experimenting with different photographic angles and equipment. The job may pay well, and the work is creative.

Learning Experiences

1. Using a wallpaper sample book, find three different types of patterns in wallpaper, all of which use the same basic color scheme.
2. Make a list of your three favorite colors. Next, design a color scheme for a room that does *not* use any of these colors but one that you could still enjoy.
3. Use watercolors or tempera paints to:
   a) mix colors for a color wheel using only the primary colors. Then, mix twenty-four hues. When dry, cut and mount them.
   b) mix your own favorite color and two accent colors to go with it.
   c) mix six tints and six shades from a hue of medium intensity.
4. Choose a color photograph of a room design, and create a totally different color scheme for that room. Using color swatches and fabric samples, describe where and how you would use your colors to replace the ones in the photograph.
5. Take two color chips, one of a primary color in intense value and one of a tertiary color in a tint. Look at the chips in each of the following lights:
   a) morning light in an east window
   b) afternoon light in an east window
   c) afternoon light in a west window
   d) incandescent light of 40 watts, 60 watts, and 100 watts
   e) florescent light
   How does light affect color?

3
CHAPTER

Establishing a Background

The next time you enter a room that is new to you, check yourself to see what you notice first. Is it a piece of furniture, a picture, or a lamp? What you probably will *not* notice at first are the walls, floors, and ceilings. Unless the wallpaper is very dramatic or the rug very unusual, you scarcely see large areas. While the walls, floor, ceiling, and woodwork all contribute to the overall impression a room makes on a person, they are generally not planned to call attention to themselves. For this reason, these elements are called *backgrounds*. In most room designs, their job is to provide an attractive, harmonious setting for the room's furnishings.

Because you think your stay in some of the homes in which you will live may be rather brief, you may feel it is unnecessary and unwise to spend much money changing room backgrounds. After all, the floors, walls, and ceilings are large areas. The costs in labor and material of doing anything to them can be high. However, a change does not always have to be expensive. If the color or condition of walls, ceilings, or floors is bad, the landlord may be glad to furnish the materials for improvement if you will do the work. A day or two of work with quick-drying paint, inexpensive wallpaper, or easily-laid floor covering can pay big dividends. The room itself, as well as the furnishings in it, will look better.

As An Important Feature. Sometimes, the walls, ceiling, floor, or woodwork of a room are designed to be that room's most important feature. Some old houses have ceilings that are decorated with elaborate and delicate plasterwork. A room design can be planned that will make such a ceiling the room's most eye-catching feature. Other old homes have elaborately carved door and window frames, chair rails, and baseboards. In these homes, the woodwork should be highlighted as the most important feature. Occasionally, the walls are the most important feature. For example, in many bathrooms the walls offer the only real opportunity to make a strong decorating statement. In cases where a background is to be featured, the room's other elements should be quiet and low-key in effect. In that way, they will not detract from the main feature of the room.

As A True Background. But walls, ceilings, floors, and woodwork will not usually be the focal point of your design scheme. Instead, you will want them to serve as true backgrounds. They should be attractive, of course. But they will be planned to help the room's furnishings show off to best advantage.

As Personal Expression. Backgrounds have another function, too. They help to establish the room's personality. Every room has a personality. It tells a story about the people who live in it, giving a subtle message of what they are like. Some rooms create an impression of quiet, formal elegance. Other rooms suggest a casual informality. Does the room suggest that the person who lives in it is vibrant and energetic—or more thoughtful and sensitive? Does the room suggest a sophisticated coolness, or does it suggest a homespun warmth? Much of the impression created depends on the room's background. For this reason, in designing a room you need to keep clearly in mind the kind of personality you want to convey. A skilled designer can make almost any room express any personality. Of course, there are limits. But, within a broad, general range, any room can be made more or less formal, more or less snug, more or less sophisticated. For example, a room whose backgrounds are in coarse textures and in earthy colors (such as yellows, browns, and rusts) will look warm and cozy and countrified. If the walls are covered in smooth paper and the background colors are blues, violets, and grays, that same room will seem less warm and cozy.

For this reason, you should have a clear sense of the personality you wish your design to convey before you begin making choices about the room's background elements.

PLANNING FLOOR TREATMENTS

The cost of floor covering is usually greater than that of any other background area. So it is natural to begin a room scheme by planning the floor.

Red-cedar paneling creates an appropriate rustic background for a free-standing fireplace, rugs, wallhangings, and basketry. The combination establishes a Native American design theme.

Another reason to begin with a decision about floor covering is that design choices for floor treatments are more limited than for other background areas. After you choose the floor covering, you can then work around it as you make choices for the other background areas of your room.

Wood Floors

Many people find the look of natural-wood floors very appealing. This is particularly true of parquet (pronounced par-KAY) floors, in which different shades of wood are used to create geometric patterns.

Refinishing. The condition of the floor is an important consideration. Is it in good enough shape to be used as is? Or must it be refinished? If the wood is basically in good condition but has an unattractive surface, the top can be sanded down. Sanding will reveal the bare wood underneath and smooth out any minor imperfections in the wood's surface. Refinishing a floor is a time-consuming job. But it is not an impossible task for the do-it-yourselfer with a rented floor-sanding machine. Once the floor has been sanded, it can be stained to match or complement the furniture you will be using. Natural-wood floors are a suitable and attractive background for almost any kind of room furnishings. In warm climates, wood floors also add a cooling look. On the other hand, wood floors need to be waxed regularly if they are to look their best. Not everyone is willing to devote the time necessary to their upkeep.

Painting. Another treatment for wood floors that are in bad shape is to paint them. There are several ways to paint floors effectively. All of them begin by

The high costs of and limited choices available for floor treatments usually make floor coverings the first design decision. Hard floor coverings include ceramic and vinyl tiles, linoleum, and the wood parquet being put down in this picture.

COLOR AND DESIGN

The best source of timelessly beautiful color combinations is nature. Natural landscapes can teach us about how colors work together. Think of the color schemes of the brilliant autumn forest, the fragile pastels and sand tones of the desert, and the range of intense blues and greens found at the ocean shore.

Color Wheels

Direct complement

The Triad

Split complement

The Monochromatic

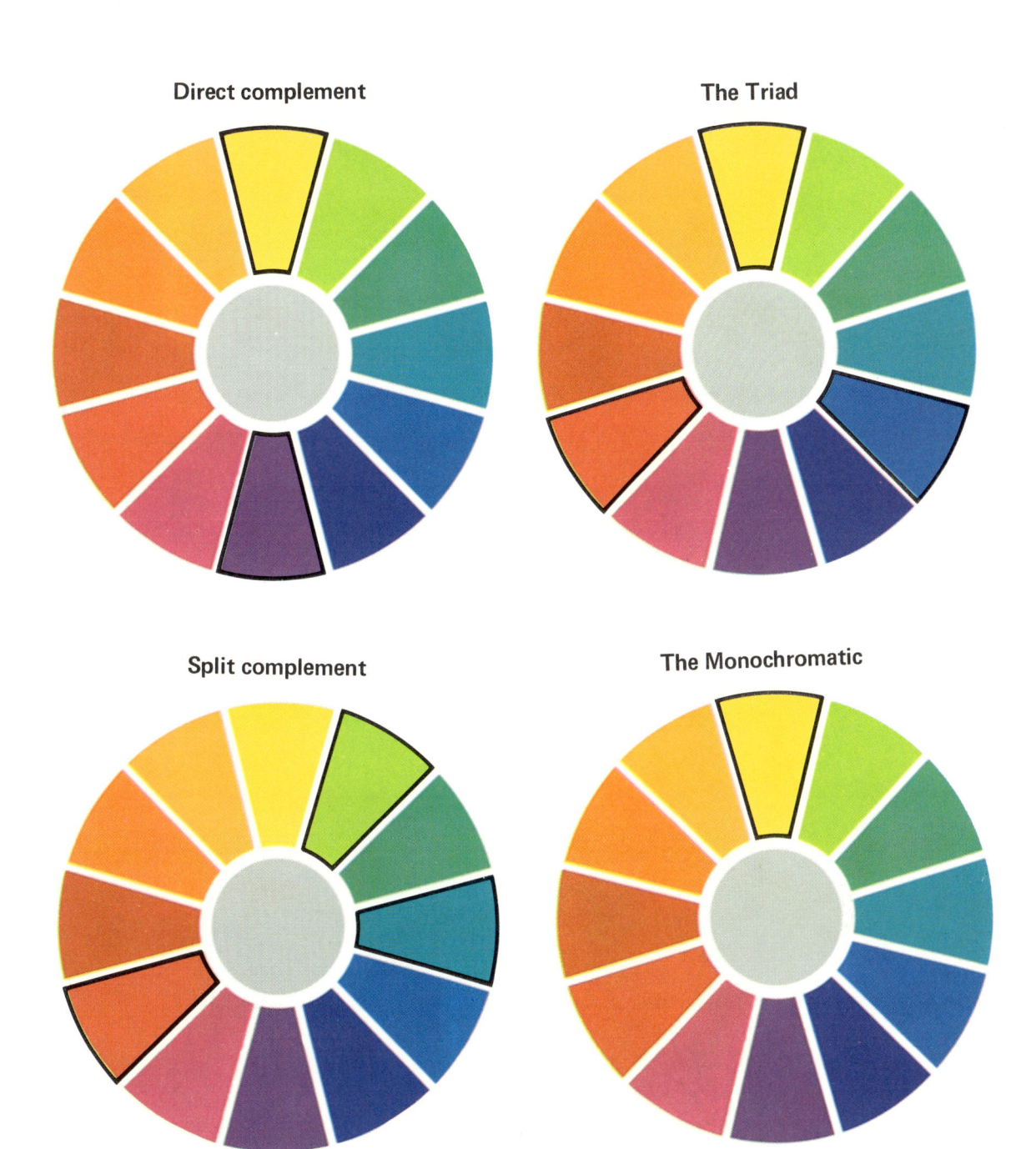

The standard color wheel with twelve colors is useful in identifying effective color combinations. (A) Complementary color schemes are those colors which are directly opposite one another on the color wheel. (B) Split complementary-color schemes form a three-part harmony in which the colors on either side of a color are used with its complementary color. (C) Triadic color schemes are three-color harmonies in which the colors are all equidistant on the color wheel. (D) Monochromatic color schemes make use of one-color harmonies, using one color in different values and intensities and one neutral in various values.

The monochromatic color scheme here combines several shades of the cream-colored and beige-toned furnishings and floor covering with the accent of colorful throw pillows.

An analogous color scheme of red, violet, and mauve was chosen to blend with the dominant neutral color of the carpeting.

A complimentary color scheme of red and green dramatizes the rugged simplicity of a bedroom.

The triadic color scheme of red, yellow, and blue serves as a dramatic and colorful design element in this attractive dining area.

Color Schemes

Function in Design

Special interests often provide unusual design and accessories. The design of this hobby workroom, with its display shelves, library, and work area, expresses its use as a space for display of the owner's rock collection.

Floor Covering in Design

This neutral-colored sisal carpet gives this living area a sense of space. The furnishings seem to stand apart from each other, almost to float in the space. Adding a different floor covering changes the room's focus. The colorfully patterned area rug gives unity to the room and its furnishings.

Art in Design

The neutral background colors of artist Robert Motherwell's living room highlights the many works of art displayed on every wall.

An Oriental-type area rug adds visual interest to this living-room arrangement. Soft floor coverings, such as wall-to-wall carpeting and large area rugs, are also excellent heat insulators. Is this room more appealing to you with or without the rug?

covering the floor with a coat of solid-color paint in the dominant color of the room. The floor can then be *spattered* (have paint of contrasting color dribbled on it). Or it can be stencilled with a design that uses contrasting color. The floor can also be painted with a wide border of contrasting color, suggesting a rug. Painted floors are especially effective with informal, countrified settings. Like natural-wood floors, they tend to look cool.

There are disadvantages to painting floors, however. Paint tends to wear unevenly. So high-traffic areas can quickly become soiled and dingy. Painted floors also tend to assume a great deal of visual importance, even when they are painted in dark neutral colors. Perhaps this is because they are so unusual. Another disadvantage is that redecorating a painted floor can be a major chore. Sometimes, it is necessary to remove the entire painted surface, even if you only wish to paint the floor again. Paint chips, cracks, and flecks in the first surface must be sanded smooth before repainting.

Sealing. There are several kinds of sealers that can be used on wood floors that are stained or painted. These sealers help to protect the wood surfaces from wear

Energy Tips

A rug helps insulation by helping to keep warm or cool air inside a room. A pad under the rug saves even more energy. Wall-to-wall carpeting is better insulation than a throw rug or wood, tile, slate, or resilient floor coverings. The carpeting prevents cold drafts from entering the room through cracks where the floor and wall join. In general, the thicker and denser the fabric of the carpet or rug, the more energy it saves. For insulation, the best fibers are wool and acrylic; the least effective fiber is nylon.

and to make cleaning them easier. Not all sealers are suitable for interior use, however. Some of them give floors a high *gloss*, or shine, which some people find unattractive. Others have a low-gloss or "satin" finish. If you are considering wood floors for your home, it would be wise to investigate these products. One of them might be suited to your needs.

Hard Floor Coverings

A variety of manufactured floor coverings made of hard materials is available, including ceramic tiles, vinyl tiles, linoleum, and prefinished plywood parquet. Such floor coverings have become very popular in recent years. Of all floor coverings, the hard coverings are the easiest to keep clean and bright and the most durable. They withstand heavy traffic and are usually easy to install. Square self-adhesive tiles are popular with "do-it-yourselfers." A wide range of colors, patterns, and designs is available in a wide range of prices.

One objection to the hard floor coverings from a design point of view is that they are cold. In general, they are not only cold to the touch but cold in appearance. Some people do not like getting out of a warm bed and putting their feet on a hard floor covering. These same people would probably not enjoy sitting on a hard floor covering to listen to records either. For this reason, hard floor coverings are often used in kitchens and bathrooms but not in living rooms and bedrooms unless combined with area rugs. If ease of maintenance is a priority, however, don't discard the idea of hard floor coverings too quickly. A little searching in the stores could lead you to the right choice of hard floor covering for the room you are designing.

Soft Floor Coverings

Probably the widest variety of floor coverings falls into the soft category. Soft floor coverings are the most popular choice for today's homes. No matter what color you wish to use, no matter what feeling or mood you wish to create, no matter what your budget limitations are, you are sure to find a soft floor covering that will suit your purposes.

There are many different elements to be considered when choosing a soft floor covering. A helpful way to evaluate any possibility is to consider these three elements: type, fiber, and style of construction.

Types. The type of any woven floor covering is determined by the size and kind of loom on which it was produced. (Obviously, this applies only to rugs and other soft coverings that are made on looms. But most soft coverings fall into this category.) A *rug* or *area rug* is a stock-sized floor covering smaller than the room in which it is used. Rugs are available in a wide variety of sizes. Some area rugs are no larger than mats, while others are nearly room-sized. A rug will often have a decorative edging which binds the rug's fabric and prevents it from unraveling. Often, this edging will take the form of a fringe.

Carpet is the term given to floor coverings woven by the yard on a loom that is 274.32, 365.76, 457.2, or 548.64 centimeters (9, 12, 15, or 18 feet) wide. Sometimes, such carpeting is called *broadloom*. This is because the loom on which it was woven was broad in width. But the term *broadloom* indicates

LOOPED WEAVES

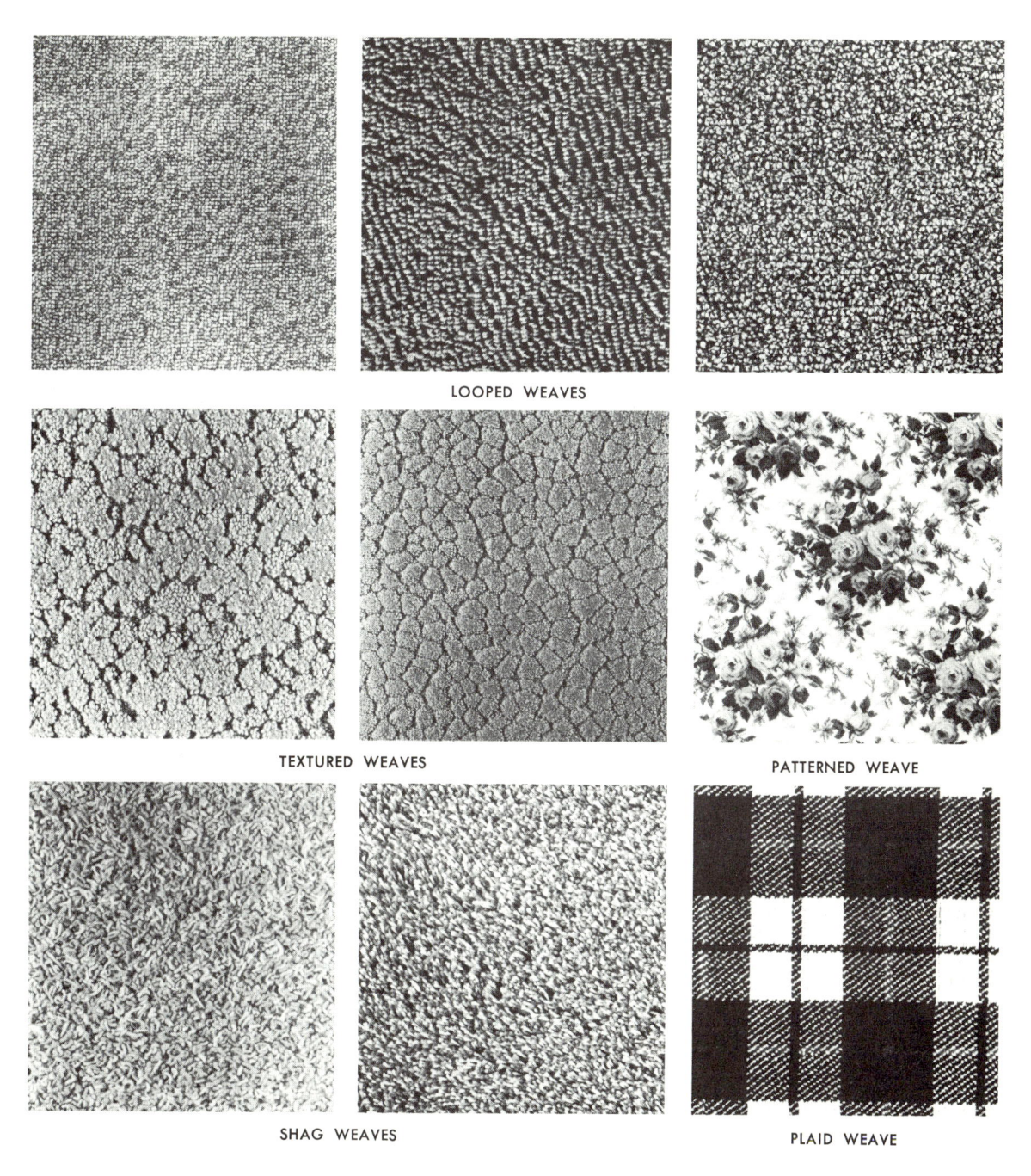

TEXTURED WEAVES

PATTERNED WEAVE

SHAG WEAVES

PLAID WEAVE

Types of Carpeting

Soft floor coverings are the most popular choice for today's home. Carpeting is available in a wide variety of colors, patterns, and fibers. It is woven on a loom by the yard into various sizes and weaves. Which weave appeals to you most?

Beauty of design and quality of workmanship make handcrafted rugs popular design choices. What factors should you take into account before buying a handcrafted rug?

nothing about the quality of the carpet. Carpeting woven on large looms can be cut and bound to make rugs of any size. Its chief use is to cover the floor of a room completely. When carpet is used this way, none of the room's floor shows. The carpet runs from wall to wall and is therefore called "wall-to-wall carpeting." Such installations can be expensive, however. This is because in cutting the carpeting to fit a particular room, there is frequently much waste. In addition, the carpet cannot be turned to even the wear. When a part of the carpet becomes worn, the entire carpet needs to be replaced.

A *runner* is a narrow carpet woven by the yard on a loom 819.96 or 1079.28 centimeters (27 or 36 inches) wide. Runners are used primarily in hallways and on stairs. But runners can be sewed together to make area rugs or room-sized rugs.

Carpet squares are squares of carpeting that can be installed by do-it-yourselfers. Carpet squares are backed with a self-gluing surface and are installed checkerboard fashion. An advantage of this type of carpeting is that worn or damaged areas can be removed. Replacing carpet squares involves minimal effort and expense. A possible disadvantage, however, is that the seams of the squares create a checkerboard pattern unless it is hidden by a deep pile or a design. Such a pattern is not suitable to many types of room design.

Fibers. The fiber content of carpets is very important. What a carpet is made of will affect not only its appearance but also its durability and ease of maintenance. Originally, all floor coverings were made of natural fibers. Today, the popularity of natural fibers has been diminished by the newer, less-expensive manufactured fibers. But natural-fiber carpeting is often the first choice if cost is not a factor. Wool carpeting has the greatest durability and *resiliency,* or "bounciness." Wool takes deep, rich dye colors and holds them especially well. The two highest-quality wools used in carpeting today are sheep's wool and *mohair* (goat's wool) imported from Argentina. The price of such floor coverings is high and the quantity is limited. In addition to its cost, wool carpeting has other disadvantages. It is faded by strong sunlight, and it is a conductor of static electricity. People who walk across a wool carpet may get a small electric shock when they touch a metal door handle or light switch.

Silk is another fiber used in natural-floor coverings. It too holds rich colors very well and, like wool, is very costly. Silk is generally used only in the most expensive Oriental area rugs. Because of the fineness of the fiber, it is usually woven into extremely delicate designs. But the fiber's fineness means that silk rugs do not withstand wear well. For this reason, silk rugs are used for wall hangings rather than for floor coverings.

Cotton floor coverings are available in a wide variety of colors and sizes. They are also relatively inexpensive. Cotton floor coverings, however, have little resiliency. They tend to mat down and do not have the "give" underfoot that more-expensive types of floor coverings have. Also, cotton soils quickly. For these reasons, area rugs of cotton are usually chosen in small sizes, so that they can be washed easily.

Other natural fibers occasionally used in floor coverings are grass, rushes, and wood pulp. Floor coverings of these fibers give a room a very light, summery feeling. They are often chosen for use on porches and in summer houses. These floor coverings are not especially durable, however, nor are they highly stain-resistant. Thus they do not stand up to long, hard use. On the other hand, they have the advantage of low cost. Machine-made matting is very inexpensive. Also, there is no question that they can add a great deal of textural interest to a room. In some circumstances, these natural floor coverings are the ideal decorating choice. For example, a bedroom with Oriental decor would probably benefit greatly from the use of Japanese *tatami* (woven straw) mats on the floor.

Synthetics. Since early in this century, the natural fibers have been supplemented by manufactured fibers—the *synthetics*. Among the most popular synthetics are nylon, acrylic, polyester, olefin, modacrylic, and rayon. Synthetic fibers were developed by chemists in laboratories and are now extremely important in the manufacture of floor coverings. Synthetics can either be used alone or in combination with a natural fiber, such as wool. There are many advantages to a floor covering made of synthetic fibers. Synthetic fibers are mildew resistant, and waterborne stains can be removed from them easily. (Oil-borne stains, however, can be hard to remove.) Synthetic floor coverings are highly durable and require little maintenance. They are available in an almost infinite variety of colors and textures. Another advantage of the synthetics is that they are generally less expensive than wool. Despite these advantages, some people feel that synthetics simply do not have the warmth or luxurious softness of wool.

Construction and Design. The way in which a floor covering is constructed affects its beauty, durability, and cost. And almost impossible to separate from style of construction is the artistry that has gone into the design of a floor covering's color, pattern, and texture.

The honeycomb texture of this synthetic carpeting creates a light and dark pattern similar to early handcrafted rugs.

Handmade. The first floor coverings were made by hand, and this tradition has survived to the present day. Perhaps the most treasured of the handmade rugs are those in which each individual loop of thread is inserted and tied by hand. Oriental rugs are made this way. Rugs are still made this way in Scandinavia. Hand-tied pile rugs with beautiful designs are much in demand. They are always very expensive, but they keep their value. Antique Oriental rugs are so much in demand that even when they are nearly threadbare they sell for high prices. Such rugs have proved a good investment for those who could afford them. They also provide a background of great elegance for almost any room.

A variety of needlework styles have been used in handmade rugs. For instance, needlepoint and cross-stitch rugs have long been popular. They can be timelessly beautiful if well designed. But the amount of labor involved in their manufacture tends to make them very expensive. You can make one yourself, but the cost of materials will still make the rug expensive. One type of needlework rug that is not too expensive is the Numdah rug from India. Numdah rugs have delicate floral patterns embroidered on a fabric of felted goat's hair.

Hooked and braided rugs originated as an economy in rural parts of Europe and America. Worn clothing was cut into strips. The strips were then either hooked into a canvas backing, or braided, coiled, and sewn to make oval area rugs. Such rugs tend to be sturdy. They are good choices when you want to give a room a casual or countrified look.

The rag rug is another kind of rug originally created to save money. Strips of old cloth (the rags) were woven into the heavy warp threads on a loom. Rag rugs usually were woven without a pattern. The pattern of the finished rug was created by the haphazard variation of colors of the rags. Rag rugs are a style of flat-woven rug. Another flat-woven area rug is the tapestry rug. In tapestry rugs, a specific pattern is woven into the rug with differently colored yarns. French

Savonnerie rugs of the eighteenth century are examples of elegant tapestry rugs. Native American rugs are examples of dramatic tapestry rugs.

Today, many hobbyists and craftspeople make their own floor coverings in the old rugmaking styles. There are many books available that describe various rugs you can make yourself. Hobby and craft shops can supply these books, as well as kits you can use for rug-making. But making a rug requires a great deal of time and effort. It can be expensive, as well. If you decide to make a rug, be sure to pick a design that will please you for a long time.

Machine-Made. Machine-made rugs and carpets are generally less expensive than the handmade varieties. Their lower cost makes them the choice of many consumers today. Developments in the floor-covering field have kept pace with consumers' needs and interests. You can find machine-made floor coverings that nearly duplicate the look of handmade floor coverings.

Some machine-made floor coverings have a *pile*. Pile is fiber that stands up from the backing of the rug or carpet. It is woven at the same time as the backing itself. Other floor coverings are made by a tufting process. Rows of pile yarn are sewed to a separate backing material. The texture of machine-made pile rugs is produced by cutting or leaving uncut the loops of the pile. Another texturing method involves twisting the pile. Varying the color of the yarns used in the pile also creates texture. Pattern is sometimes put into a one-color rug by cutting some of the looped pile or by cutting the tufts at different heights. And, of course, pattern is also put into rugs by weaving colored yarns in set designs.

Manufacturers of soft floor coverings often recommend the use of a special pad beneath the floor covering itself. These pads are usually quite inexpensive. They repay their cost by extending the life of the carpet or rug by years.

PLANNING WALL TREATMENTS

Historically, walls were built of clay, stone, or wood. They were hung with tapestries for additional warmth. Some were painted with whitewash. Others

Wall-to-wall carpeting is a popular design choice for warm and comfortable floors. Although costly to install, it is energy-efficient.

The craft of weaving, used to make both wall-hangings and rugs, is an ancient tradition that has recently been revived in the country. Many people have taken up weaving as a hobby or a job.

were covered by fabric stretched between thin wooden supports. In palaces, this fabric covering was often silk damask, cut velvet, and printed linen. In cottages, it was usually cotton, printed with one color.

Painted scenic wallpaper originated in the Orient. It was imported, at great expense, by people in Europe and America. But eventually, European and American manufacturers began to copy both the Oriental scenic wallpapers and the European provincial fabric wall coverings. These imitations were produced in the form of inexpensive wallpapers. Paint companies began to produce wall paint with color in it, to replace the earlier whitewash for walls. Lumber mills began making plywood panels that imitated more-expensive wood-paneled walls. Today, we have a great range of wall coverings from which to choose in designing attractive rooms.

Paint

Perhaps the most flexible wall covering is paint. The cost of painting depends upon the type and quality of paint you choose. It also depends upon whether you do the painting yourself or pay someone to do it.

Types of Paint. Most paint is either *oil-based, latex,* or *acrylic*. The terms refer to the substance that holds the colored pigment. Oil-based paints are durable, but they tend to be expensive. Many of the latex and acrylic paints are far less expensive. These paints have other advantages, too. They are easy to apply. They are also less likely than oil-based paints to show brush marks. They also stand up to washing very well, often better than oil-based paints do.

Choosing Paints. The kind of paint you choose will depend somewhat upon the kind of surface you are going to cover. All readily available types of paint can be used over wood or plaster. But certain paints have been manufactured to cover other types of surfaces. (If you plan to paint a wall that has been papered, you must be willing to remove all the wallpaper first.) It is wise to discuss your particular situation with the salesperson where you buy the paint. She or he should be able to advise you about which paint will meet your particular needs.

Paint is a very popular choice among interior designers. This is partly because paint can be purchased in a virtually endless array of colors to match any color scheme. But paint is also popular because, more than any other wall covering, it makes walls a true background for beautiful room furnishings. Painted walls are generally less likely to attract attention to themselves than walls treated in other ways.

Wallpaper

Wallpapers are available in almost every conceivable style, texture, design, and color combination. For that reason, they are also a popular wall-covering

Top: The room on the left shows a natural value color relationship with darker values on the floor, lighter values on the walls, and lightest values on the ceiling. Shifting this order, as in the room on the right, produces more-dramatic effects. *Bottom:* These rooms show different ways of establishing a dominant color.

choice. One advantage of wallpaper over paint is that paper, if it is rough-textured or patterned, will hide minor surface imperfections in the walls. Major surface imperfections, however, must be fixed before wallpaper is applied.

Wallpaper Surfaces. Today, most wallpapers have smooth surfaces. But there are enough textured papers on the market to give the interior designer a real choice. Many textured papers are *embossed* to look like canvas, linen, silk, tweed, or grasscloth. Embossing raises certain sections of the paper from the background, generally to highlight some element in the design. These papers offer interesting textural effects that you might find suitable to a particular room scheme. (There are also wall coverings made of actual canvas, silk, grasscloth, and linen. But these coverings tend to be extremely expensive. They are also more difficult to hang.) Another advantage of textured papers is that they generally have a random, all-over pattern. This means they do not require matching from roll to roll and from seam to seam. So there is little waste when using a textured paper.

Wallpaper Patterns. The range of patterned wallpapers is almost inexhaustible. Most patterned papers are machine printed. But some of the more expensive papers are hand-blocked, embossed, or flocked. Flocking covers certain elements of the design with fabric fibers. These fibers make the design look and feel somewhat like thin velvet.

Other special papers include those that are coordinated with fabric. Both the fabric and the wallpaper are printed with identical colors and designs. Thus, they may be used together in complete harmony. There are also mural wallpapers. The murals look like realistic paintings and are printed on the paper. They can show a landscape, trees, or a city skyline. You can use these papers to cover a whole wall (or a large section of a wall) with just one large picture. There are even papers designed to resemble architectural elements of a room. For example, there are papers that look like pillars, panels, moldings, and so on.

Most wallpapers, however, are simply printed with an all-over repeated design. There will be many books of samples of such papers in the wallpaper department of a store near you. When choosing wallpaper, be sure you keep in mind your color scheme and the scale or size of the room. This will ensure that the paper you choose will be harmonious with the rest of the room.

Other special wallpapers you should know about are those that have been given a special vinyllike surface. These wallpapers can easily be scrubbed clean. Thus, they are particularly suitable for kitchens and bathrooms, where splashes and spots can quickly ruin an ordinary paper wallcovering.

If you are a willing do-it-yourselfer, you may want to try using *prepasted* wallpapers. These papers are backed with a special paste. You activate the paste by dipping the paper in water. Then it is ready to hang. (Of course, you can also hang papers that are not prepasted. You can get advice and the necessary equipment from your wallpaper store.) "Strippable" wallpapers are also available. These papers can be removed (stripped) from walls easily. This is a definite advantage when the time comes to redecorate a room.

Paint is the most widely used wall covering. It is easy to apply and, if you do it yourself, can be relatively inexpensive.

Sheathing

Prefinished or unfinished plywood panels can be used to *sheath* (cover) walls. This technique is particularly useful where wall surfaces have many cracks, chips, and other serious flaws. Such panels are also a popular choice for game rooms, dens, and other informal family rooms.

Prefinished plywood is produced in a wide range of wood finishes. It is fairly easy to install and quite easy to care for. But the installation is generally regarded as semipermanent. Therefore, be sure to choose paneling that will please you for a long time. Unfinished plywood is less expensive than the prefinished kind. But you must put a finish on it yourself. Unfinished plywood can be painted or stained in a natural-wood stain. It can even be papered. One very practical benefit of sheathing is that it acts as additional insulation for a room.

Fabric

Recently, there has been a trend toward using fabric as a wallcovering. The fabric can be pasted directly on the walls themselves. Or it can be stapled to thin

---

Energy Tips

Vinyl wallpaper is especially effective for blocking drafts and for insulating cold walls. Other wall coverings that may serve as insulation against cold air are: large pictures, Oriental screen panels, tapestries, and wall carpeting.

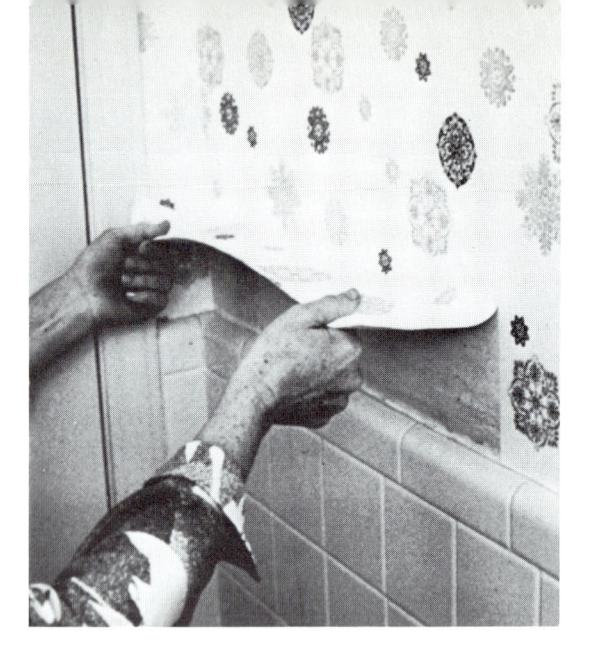

Wallpaper today has the decorating advantage of being easy to apply and easy to remove. Special vinyl papers, which wipe clean, have been developed for kitchen and bath use.

wooden strips that have first been fastened to the walls. A third method is to stretch the fabric on rods. The rods themselves are fastened to the walls near the ceiling and baseboards. It takes many yards of fabric to cover a wall. So this approach tends to be costly, except for very small rooms.

Different Effects. The usual way to use any of these wall coverings is to cover all of the walls of a room in the same way. But there are other possibilities. In certain circumstances, one of these alternatives could be even more effective. For example, some rooms have one wall that is a natural focal point. It may be a fireplace wall. It may be one unbroken wall against which it would be natural to center a large piece of furniture. Or it may be a "gallery wall" for hanging a collection of paintings and other objects. It is often effective to treat these "special" walls differently from the other walls in the room. The fireplace wall, for instance, might be covered with wood sheathing, and the rest of the walls might be papered. The gallery wall might be painted in one color, while the other walls in the room might be painted in a different color or covered with a patterned paper. The wall behind a double bed could be papered in a particularly dramatic pattern. The remaining walls could be painted a solid, neutral color taken from the paper's color scheme. Of course, not every room has one wall that cries out for special treatment. You should avoid giving special treatment to a wall that is not important. But don't discard this idea without considering its possibilities for your room first.

PLANNING CEILING TREATMENTS

Ask almost anyone the question: "What color is a ceiling?" Nine times out of ten you will get the answer: "White." There is nothing wrong with a plain white ceiling, of course. In many cases that will be your choice. But a ceiling doesn't *have* to be plain white. Ceilings are not generally as important as the walls and floor. But ceilings do have a role to play in creating the background impression of a room. Therefore, their treatment should be given careful thought.

Quiet Ceilings. If a ceiling is in good condition, painting is the easiest way to treat it. If you want it to be *unobtrusive* (of almost no importance), paint it with a color that is light in value. If you are also painting the walls, you can mix a little of the wall color in with the ceiling paint. This trick ensures that the ceiling color will blend with the wall color. There are other ways to make the ceiling unobtrusive. You could paint it exactly the same color as the walls. Or you could paper the ceiling with the same wallpaper you are using in the rest of the room. Papering a ceiling has the effect of "lowering" it or making the room feel smaller.

If the ceiling is in poor condition, it is generally easier to cover it than to repair it. Sheathing can be used to cover a ceiling. Ceiling tiles can also be used. Three kinds of overhead tiles are available. The *interlocking style* is stapled to the ceiling. Another kind is attached to the ceiling with *mastic,* or special paste which is a type of cement. The third kind is a *drop-in tile*. Drop-in tiles are designed to rest on a special metal frame fastened to the walls just below the old ceiling. All three of these types of tiles come in various sizes, textures, and colors. Any of them can be readily repainted.

Dramatic Ceilings. But suppose you don't want your ceiling to be unobtrusive? An easy way to add color to a room that needs a bit of "zip" is to repeat the color and value of the room's rug on the ceiling. This treatment is often dramatic and exciting. It makes a room unusual. A patterned paper on the ceiling can effectively liven up a room with a plain floor and walls. Another possibility,

Plywood paneling is often applied to the walls of informal game and family rooms. The wood sheathing is very durable and fairly easy to install.

especially attractive in bedrooms with wallpaper that is realistically patterned, is to cut a few of the design motifs (elements) from the wallpaper itself. Then paste these cut-outs in an interesting arrangement on the ceiling. You can cluster them over the head of the bed, for example. Or you can encircle the ceiling light fixture with them.

A special kind of problem with which you may have to deal is the slanted ceiling. If the room is built up under the eaves of the house, its ceiling and walls will meet each other at various angles. One effective way to handle this kind of room is to treat the walls and ceiling as one surface. By painting them both the same color or by papering both with a wallpaper that uses a small pattern, you can hide the lines where the walls and ceiling meet. Such a treatment will give the room a sense of unity. It will also mask the diagonal lines that would otherwise call attention to the room's odd shape.

PLANNING WOODWORK TREATMENTS

Many rooms have some woodwork in them. Rooms may have baseboards, door and window frames, and moldings where walls join ceiling. In planning for a room, you need to decide how to handle the woodwork.

In most cases, you will choose to make woodwork as unobtrusive as possible. In a painted room, this can be done by painting the woodwork the same color as the walls. In a papered room, paint the woodwork a color to match the background of the wallpaper.

But suppose the woodwork of the room is beautiful. You may not want to hide it at all. You might even choose to make it a focal point of attention. If so, you would paint or stain the woodwork in a color that will make it stand out from the walls. Or, you may want to refinish the woodwork to enhance its beauty.

Ornately carved woodwork is often seen in older homes and apartment buildings. Its elegant beauty suggests a formality not found in contemporary homes.

Adding Woodwork. You may want to *add* woodwork to a room, to give it additional character. Attaching a heavy wooden molding at about table height on all of the walls is an inexpensive and effective way to create a dado or to accent a room. Or you might use strips of wood molding to create a panel on a wall behind an important piece of furniture. Another possibility is to add a ceiling molding. This is a strip of carved wood fastened to the wall at the point where the wall joins the ceiling. Or you might even want to add false beams to a ceiling. They are lightweight and can be attached with mastic. Today, all sorts of imitation architectural elements are available at your local building-supply store.

SHOPPING FOR BACKGROUND MATERIALS

Whether you are designing a real room, one which you actually intend to redecorate or are designing a "room in your head"—an imaginary "dream" room—the experience of actually going into stores and shops to look for products that will fit your design scheme can be a fascinating one. You may find the experience bewildering at first. You will be confronted by an endless variety of possibilities from which to choose. But the very process of beginning to make those choices will be helpful to you. As you talk with salespeople who are knowledgeable about interior design, you will gradually sharpen and clarify your design sense. That will help you as you have increasing opportunities to make purchasing decisions.

What You Need

To be an effective shopper for any home furnishings project, you need to be a prepared shopper. You need a great deal of detailed, accurate information. For example, to shop intelligently for materials, you need the following:

A Floorplan of Your Room. This drawing will show the arrangement of walls. It should also carry notations of the room's dimensions (height, length, and width). In addition, the floorplan should show the placement and dimensions of all doors and windows. The placement of such fixtures as radiators, light switches, electrical outlets, and so on should also be noted on the floorplan.

Your Proposed Color Scheme. If possible, take with you samples of the exact colors you want to use. It is nearly impossible to match colors from memory. You can provide yourself with color swatches, or samples, in any of several ways. Find small objects that are the right color and take them with you when you shop. Cut color samples and pictures out of magazines. The form your color swatches take doesn't matter. What matters is that you have exact samples of the colors you want to use.

Clear Knowledge of Your Decorating Budget. Knowing exactly how much money you can spend on your background materials is very important. There is nothing wrong with visiting stores on a "just looking" basis at first. But when you are seriously trying to choose materials for purchase, your trip will be far more productive if you have a clear idea of your own financial limits. Preparation will save you and the salespeople who help you time and frustration.

FLOOR COVERINGS

Type	Size	Use	Special Qualities
CARPETING			
Broadloom Standard indoor	12 and 15 feet	Wall-to-wall installation Cut into room or area-sized rugs Cut into runners	
Exceptional indoor	12, 15, 18 feet		Good for use in especially wide rooms
Indoor-outdoor	3, 6, 9, 12 feet	Outdoors and indoors in areas of hard wear, such as kitchen, bath, halls	Moisture, spot- and soil-resistant
Runners Standard indoor	27 and 36 inches	Halls and stairways	Available only in commercial quantities
Hemp	27 inches	Halls and stairways	Imported from India and occasionally available in home lengths
RUGS			
Small Area rugs	24 by 36 inches 27 by 48 inches 24 by 70 inches 3 by 5 feet	Accent or area emphasis	
Large Area and room-sized	6 by 9 feet 9 by 12 feet 12 by 15 feet	Area rugs in large rooms All-over carpeting effect in small rooms	
SQUARES			
Fiber	18 by 18 inches 12 by 12 inches	Sewed together to form area or room-sized rugs Use with metal or reed furniture	Imported from Orient
Carpet	12 by 12 inches	Cemented together for floors and walls— indoors and outdoors	Easy replacement
RUG PADDING			
Sponge rubber waffle mold	Same as rug or carpeting	Gives softness and longer wear to floor coverings	Extra buoyancy
Smooth rubber solid sponge	Same as rug or carpeting	Gives softness and longer wear to floor coverings	Hard wearing
Cattle hair and fiber	Same as rug or carpeting	Gives softness and longer wear to floor coverings	Less expensive
Hair and sponge rubber	Same as rug or carpeting	Gives softness and longer wear to floor coverings	

A Notebook and Pencil. You are going to collect a great deal of information about floor coverings, paints, fabrics, and paneling materials on your shopping trip. Much of this information will be necessary when you are making your final purchase decisions. The importance of writing this information down at the time you get it cannot be stressed too strongly. We are all tempted at times to rely on our memories to carry such data. But it is amazing how quickly we find ourselves wondering whether it was the tweed rug or the solid one that the salesperson said had to be special-ordered. Write it down!

Choosing Floor Coverings

It is logical to begin your shopping with the selection of the floor covering for two reasons. First, floor coverings are relatively expensive compared to other elements of a room's background. So it is helpful to know from the outset how much of your budget you will have to commit to this area. If the cost of floor covering is more than you expected, you can scale down your expenses for the walls and ceiling. This will be easier than cutting costs on floor coverings. The second reason to shop for floor coverings first is that possibilities in this area are more limited than for the other areas. So if you can't find a floor covering that's exactly right, it is best to find that out right away. Then you can adjust the balance of your scheme accordingly.

Questions To Ask. Floor coverings are generally long-lasting. In choosing them, think about your living situation. Will you be staying in the room you are now in for a long time? If so, you may be willing to invest in a semipermanent installation such as wall-to-wall carpeting or an expensive hard floor covering. On the other hand, if you expect to be moving within the near future, a more-movable type of floor covering would be best. Many questions about floor coverings are answered in the chart on the facing page.

Cost. Of course, you will need to think about cost. Comparison shopping between alternatives can be very helpful. Which will cost less: an area rug in a *stock size* (that is, a size that the manufacturer has predetermined) or an area rug cut from a roll to your own specifications? Can you find remnants of carpet that can be bound to serve as area rugs? If you get the largest-size rug possible, is it in a pattern that will allow you to cut the rug to fit one or more of the smaller rooms? If you will be moving, this is an important consideration. Rugs with all-over patterns or no pattern lend themselves to this economy. But rugs that have a single design which covers the entire rug cannot be cut down in this way.

Quality. No matter how much or how little money you are spending, be sure to measure cost in relation to quality. If you are spending a great deal, you have a right to expect the rug to have a high pile and a close weave. The rug should be woven of high-quality yarns or other fibers. Is the manufacturer well known, with a reputation for products that wear well? Is the store with which you are dealing a reputable firm, interested in customer satisfaction?

Upkeep. You will also want to measure cost in relation to upkeep. How much care will the floor covering that you are considering need? Pile rugs or carpets

This bedroom combines complementary textured and painted walls. The painted walls make an excellent background for paintings and other art objects.

The patchwork-look vinyl wallcovering of this informal area makes it look much more furnished than it really is. Its lively color and pattern interest also add a feeling of country warmth. How do you think other wallpaper patterns would affect this area of the room?

that are somewhat tweedy, textured, or patterned demand far less care than plain-colored ones. Any floor covering, hard or soft, in the middle-value color range will be easier to care for than those that are very light or very dark. Is mildew a problem where you live? Are moths a problem? If so, check for how well the floor covering is expected to resist those dangers.

Choosing Wall Treatments

Paint. If you have decided to use paint for your walls, check the paint samples at the hardware or paint store where you are shopping. Study the special qualities of each type of paint. (And don't be afraid to ask questions.) Then select about a half-dozen color samples that seem nearest to the one you have in mind.

Later, when you actually buy the paint, check the accuracy of the paint mixing process. Be sure the color is the one you want. Do this by applying a small amount of the mixed paint on the wall behind a piece of furniture. Or you can put it on a piece of wood that you can hold against the wall. Let the paint dry thoroughly (a heat lamp or fan can speed this process), and then check the color in different lights. It is much easier to return the paint to have the color mixture corrected than it would be to repaint the wall.

Wallpaper. In choosing wallpaper, there are certain guides to help you make your selection. If you have selected a plain or textured floor covering, you can use any type of wall treatment. But you will want to harmonize the scale (relative size) of any pattern to the size of the room where it will be used. The larger the room, the larger the wallpaper design can safely be. You will also want to choose a design that harmonizes with the mood of the room you are creating. If you want a bold, rugged room, a plaid, tweed, grasscloth, or abstract pattern would be a better choice than a floral. If you want an elegant, sophisticated room, a floral paper would be a better choice than paper with a folksy, peasant design.

Fabric. Be sure to ask the salesperson if there is a matching fabric available for any paper that interests you. Knowing that you can buy fabric that duplicates the wallpaper may help you make your decision. Such fabric can be used for curtains or shower curtains. Or it can be used as a decorative banding for bedspreads, curtains, or slipcovers. It can even be used to cover pillows. In any of these cases, use of such fabric can help to unify the look of your room.

Applied Wood. The one kind of wall covering that tends to be somewhat costly is the applied wood, or sheath type, of wall covering. If you have chosen the sheathing approach, you will need to go to a lumber yard or building-supply house. Explain your interests to the salesperson there. Ask about what materials are available. Ask how much each material costs and how it is to be applied to the wall. Paneling can be effective and less costly when used on only one wall of a room.

Regardless of the wall covering in which you are interested, be sure to explain carefully to the salesperson the kind of walls you are planning to cover. You should also describe their condition. Not every approach is appropriate, or even possible, with every kind and condition of wall. The salesperson will be able to guide you if you provide complete information.

Choosing Ceiling Treatments

The treatment you have decided upon for the ceiling will be one that has already been discussed. The same principles apply to choosing paint or wallpaper for a ceiling as apply to choosing them for walls.

BEFORE MAKING THE FINAL DECISIONS

One major step remains before you are ready actually to place an order for the necessary materials. You should take home with you samples of all the

Coordinating the floral-patterned fabric of bed covers, wall coverings, and canopy created the formal look of this bedroom.

Furnishing and decorating a room is a complex process. A knowledge of the many different elements that go into successful design will help you make right decision for your tastes and needs.

possibilities you are seriously considering. Study them in relation to one another.

Obtaining Samples. There is seldom a problem getting paint samples to take home. Most wallpaper dealers will arrange to lend you sample books to take home and study for a few days. Carpet samples are not always as easy to get. But you can usually get them if you're persistent. Or you may have to settle for a picture of the rug you are considering. But even if it is necessary to call for a sample at the time the store closes and return it as the store opens the next morning, the special effort is worth making.

How Do They Look? Spread your samples out in the room you are designing and study them carefully. How does this paint look with that piece of wallpaper? How do you like the way that rug goes with this wall color? What changes do the different elements undergo because of the particular kind and amount of light in the room? How do the samples look with any pieces of furniture you know will be part of the finished room design? Only by weighing all the different possibilities against each other will you arrive at the particular floor, wall, and ceiling treatments that satisfy you. Then you will be ready to go back to the store and say: "Thank you very much. I'll take this one."

Careers
Each county in the United States has a Cooperative Extension Service which is connected with both the United States Department of Agriculture and the local land-grant college. The function of the extension service is to provide information and advice on home- and agriculture-related topics.

In the area of home design for apartments and houses, the extension worker can provide and explain government publications about furniture and textiles. She or he teaches and counsels people on how to furnish and decorate homes, purchase and arrange furnishings, and prepare homemade furnishings. The extension worker may teach groups of people how to make curtains, reupholster furniture, or make slipcovers.

The many duties of the extension worker include traveling to community groups, presenting radio or television programs, and discussing the latest research information. The pay is good, and there are opportunities for advancement. An advantage is that a person has much freedom in planning the course of the work and hours, but irregular hours may be common.

This career requires a person who is deeply interested in people and in community well-being. The best preparation includes college courses in education and home economics.

To prepare for extension work, you can help people in your neighborhood with home projects, join a 4-H club, participate in other clubs, and visit an extension office in your county. Many offices are located within the land-grant university in the state.

Learning Experiences

1. Choose one small room in your home, and, without consideration of cost, plan how you would completely change its personality by changing its background. Select samples of your choices of paint, wallpaper or wallboard sheathing, carpeting, hard flooring, or area rugs.
2. Study other samples to see how you could obtain a similar effect for less money by using less-expensive materials. What part of the labor could you do yourself to save costs?
3. Find photographs of three different floor coverings currently available. Explain how the color, texture, and pattern of each will affect other elements in the same room. Which is easiest to care for? Which is most attractive? Which is least expensive? Which could you install yourself?
4. Prepare a bulletin-board display of photographs showing rooms or room sections in which the backgrounds—ceilings, walls, and floors—have major emphasis in the room designs.
5. Form a small committee to study and propose changes in the background treatment of your classroom. You may suggest changes in material as well as in surface finish, provided you keep in mind the practical uses to which the classroom must be put. Present your recommended scheme to the class for discussion.

CHAPTER 4

Knowing Furniture

From the beginning of civilization, people have invented and adapted objects to make basic activities such as sitting, sleeping, and eating more convenient and comfortable. No one is sure when people first began to be concerned about furniture's appearance as well as its usefulness. But certainly this development took place soon after civilization began.

Over the centuries, people became more sophisticated and their lives became more complex. Furniture became more sophisticated and complex, too. During some periods in history, the appearance of furniture was more important than its comfort and usefulness. At other times, furniture was designed for utility rather than appearance. Today, most of us want furniture that is both useful and beautiful. In fact, we find it difficult to separate *form* (how furniture looks) from *function* (how it fills our needs). When we say that we need "a good chair" or "a good table," we generally mean that we want it to be both useful and attractive.

This chapter will give you some basic information about furniture. These basic facts will help you select furniture that satisfies your own requirements for beauty and usefulness.

WHY FURNITURE DESIGN CHANGES

Furniture is meant to serve certain basic purposes. These purposes have not changed for thousands of years. But the design of furniture has changed continually throughout history. Why has this been so? There are many reasons.

Furniture Reflects Available Materials

Historically, furniture has been made of materials that were close at hand. Only in recent centuries has it been possible to use materials that come from halfway around the globe. The traditional furniture of any region reflected the wood, the metal, and the fabrics found in that area at that time. Materials, in turn, determined the design. For example, in New England when pioneers were just beginning to settle, the furniture was made of native pine. Pine lent itself to simple lines and no decoration. In France at that same time, farmers were settled and prosperous and fruit trees were everywhere. So their furniture made of these fine-grained fruit woods had curved lines and beautiful carved decoration.

Furniture Reflects Available Technology

The *technology* of a society is the combination of techniques, or ways of working with materials, existing in that society. The term *technology* also generally suggests a high use of machinery as opposed to handwork. In colonial America, tools were very simple. Almost all furniture was made by hand. So the design of early American furniture reflects that of relatively simple technology. Today, on the other hand, we live in a highly mechanical society. Most furniture now is made by machine. So the designs of much of today's furniture reflect that fact.

Furniture Reflects Life-Styles

The way we live has always dictated the basic requirements for the kind of furniture with which we live. Our personal tastes dictate which of the many different furniture designs we choose. Today, for example, the life-style of most people in the United States demands furniture that is almost maintenance-free. People do not want to spend much time dusting, waxing, and polishing furniture, or cleaning its upholstery. So manufacturers have developed furniture that needs very little care. This means furniture with surfaces that can be cleaned quickly and easily with a cloth or sponge. Easy-to-clean plastic and Formica surfaces are a common feature. Easy-care upholstery fabric has a dirt and stain resistant finish. Also, many peoples' life-style demands mobile pieces of furniture. They want furniture that can be moved easily from one home to the next. These life-style needs result in changes in the scale and design of our furniture.

In the past, life-styles were different. So furniture designs were different, too. In Victorian England, for example, people tended to have large families. Many family members lived in the family household their whole lives. Victorian furniture was often larger than today's furniture to accommodate these large families. Dining tables, for example, had to be large enough for the entire family to sit at. Bookcases had to have enough space for all the books owned by many individual family members. This furniture did not need to be moved from one home to the next.

Furniture Reflects Status

In every society, people tend to divide into definite social classes. In many societies, these classes reflect a person's economic condition. There are the rich, the middle-class, and the poor. In some societies, status is determined by education, politics, inherited titles, or royal favor.

What does all this have to do with furniture design? Many people select furniture at least partly on the basis of status.

Status today is more a decision about price than a decision about taste. People may still choose to spend a large amount of money on their furnishings in an effort to reflect a wealthy status. But their choices of the type of furnishings they buy can still be personal ones. This was not always the case.

For example, compare the present with Colonial America. In those days, everyone who could possibly manage it had Chippendale mahogany furniture. Everyone had heavy damask draperies and massive silver flatware. Everyone had Oriental rugs and English bone china. Nowadays, no one would be foolish enough to try to say what "everyone" has in furniture, draperies, rugs, flatware, or china. People now have the courage and the wisdom to set their own priorities, to choose their own way of life, and to furnish their homes to suit their own personal taste.

LINE AND SURFACE

There are two elements that contribute to the appearance of every piece of furniture. When you look at a chair, for instance, and decide you like it, you are responding to two different things about that chair which, together, determine the way it looks. Those two elements in furniture are line and surface.

Line

A piece of furniture's basic shape, or outline, is called its *line*. Are the legs of a table straight, or do they curve? Is a chest squat and solid in shape, or is it thin and delicate? The skilled interior designer looks first at a piece of furniture's lines. If a piece has "good" lines, the designer will then consider it further. If the designer decides that the piece has "bad" lines, however, that piece is usually eliminated from further consideration.

What, then, are good lines and bad lines for you? As with all questions of taste, this is essentially a personal matter. Some people like furniture with curved, delicate lines. Other people like solid, massive lines. In that sense, only you can decide whether a piece has the lines you like.

Proportion contributes to the lines of a piece of furniture. For example, imagine a dining table with a top that is 12.7 centimeters (5 inches) thick, and with legs that are thin and delicately curved. The lines of the legs may be pleasing, and the lines of the top may be pleasing. But the legs and top are not in proportion to one another. So they give the table bad lines. The relationship between different parts of a piece of furniture is as important in creating the impression of good lines for you as the actual lines themselves.

Evaluating Line. To become skilled at judging whether furniture has good or bad lines, practice looking at each piece of furniture in silhouette. You can do this by imagining that the piece of furniture is standing against a white wall that is brightly lit. This trick will help you concentrate on the shape of the furniture piece as a whole. It will also allow you to see the shape of the various parts of the piece and their relationships to each other more clearly.

Surface

The other element that contributes to how a piece of furniture looks is its surface treatment. With upholstered pieces, the surface is usually a fabric covering. With wooden pieces, the surface is the wood itself. Ask yourself if the surface treatment is appropriate to the piece as a whole. Is the surface treatment attractive in and of itself? Is the surface treatment appropriate in color, texture, and finish?

Changing Surface Treatments. Fortunately, the surface treatment of many pieces of furniture can be changed without too much effort or expense. So if you have a piece of furniture whose lines you like but whose surface displeases you, you may be able to salvage it. Slipcovers or new upholstery can improve the surface of a sofa or easy chair. A tablecloth that reaches the floor can change the surface of a small table. The surface of a wooden piece can be changed with paint. Or the old finish can be stripped off, exposing the wood itself. If you are buying a piece of new furniture, however, you might just as well shop for one with pleasing lines and an attractive surface.

Relationship of Line and Surface. How do line and surface interact? As a general rule, the more massive and crude the shape of a piece, the plainer its surface should be. Conversely, the more delicate a piece's lines, the more complicated its surface decoration may be. Country furniture is usually simple and massive in outline. Such furniture generally looks best when the wood it is made of is its only surface decoration, or if its surface can be painted to good effect. Furniture with delicate, curving lines lends itself more readily to intricate carving or decoration with inlaid designs of different colored wood pieces. Despite these general guidelines, a plain piece of furniture may sometimes be made unexpectedly beautiful by a complex surface treatment. A simple *Parson's table* (a style of table with plain, straight lines), for instance, may be finished in a mock tortoise-shell design of great subtlety and color variation.

TRADITIONAL FURNITURE

It might help to start your study of traditional styles in furniture by walking through a furniture store. Notice how much space is devoted to traditional furniture, to contemporary furniture, and to periodless furniture. Most stores have divided their stock among these three rather evenly because all three are in constant demand today.

Popularity of Traditional

The fact that traditional furniture is popular may surprise you. There are several reasons why this is true. Perhaps the most obvious one is that furniture from the past carries with it a nostalgic aura of a less-complex, less-hectic way of life than our own. It gives many people a sense of continuity and security that is very comfortable.

Another reason that many people choose traditional furniture is that they are spared from having to evaluate the value and beauty of each piece. They know that time has eliminated the mediocre and has handed down the best furniture designs of each period.

Because of the continuing popularity of certain styles of the past, many furniture manufacturers continue to make those styles available. Sometimes, manufacturers offer accurate reproductions of antique furniture. But more often, the manufacturers offer adaptations of traditional designs rather than exact

---

Energy Tips

Certain measures may be taken to achieve maximum efficiency from radiators. Be sure to dust or vacuum radiator surfaces frequently. Dust and grime impede the flow of heat. If the radiators need painting, use flat paint—preferably black. Flat paint radiates better than glossy paint.

(A) A modern French Provincial sofa adapted from the French Provincial daybed; (B) this type of high cabinet, or armoire, originally served as a bedroom closet; (C) the ladder back of the French Provincial chair has been adapted as a modern headboard; (D) the narrow form of French Provincial dining tables may be adapted as a desk or hall table; (E) the upholstered armchair is a popular modern use of French design; (F) the French Provincial ladder-back chair.

replicas of original furniture. These adaptions capture the essential look of the original antique. But the adapted pieces include some design changes to make the furniture more compatible with our present way of life. For example, today's manufacturers are producing coffee tables in early-American style. But obviously, the pioneer Americans never had coffee tables. What the manufacturers have produced are new designs that include some elements of early-American style furniture.

Every age of the past and every part of the world has special furniture designs. It would take an encyclopedia to list and describe every single style of furniture that has been developed through history. But there are a few traditional styles that have long been of particular appeal to Americans.

Provincial Furniture

The name of this type of furniture derives from the word *province*. Provinces are sections of a country that are located at some distance from that country's large cities. People of "the provinces" are, as a general rule, less sophisticated and less affluent than city people. So, provincial furniture tends to be simple and countrified. However, provincial furniture designs have often followed trends that were set in the sophisticated capital cities. So, provincial furniture is generally a simpler, more-primitive version of the furniture that was being produced in the cabinetmakers' shops of the cities of the same time and in the same country. Thus, French-provincial furniture is a country cousin of its more-sophisticated Paris equivalent, and early-American furniture tends to be a simpler version of the furniture designed and built in towns of seventeenth-century United States.

Adaptations. Today's designs based on antique provincial furniture are good choices for people who enjoy informal life-styles. Such furniture is comfortable, unpretentious, and functional. French-provincial furniture is slightly more elegant than early-American furniture. The French style features gentle curves, which many designers prefer. Despite its simplicity, French-provincial furniture does have a measure of delicacy and elegance that appeals to many people. Furniture of early-American design has its admirers, too. These people like the straightforward, rugged lines of early-American furniture.

Eighteenth-Century English and American Furniture

The masterpieces created in the furniture workshops of the large cities of England and America during the eighteenth century have elegance and grandeur. Such furniture featured fine carving and graceful proportions. It was crafted of superbly matched fine-grain woods such as mahogany, rosewood, and maple. Most of the chairs, chests, breakfronts, and cabinets were very well designed. They could serve many functions and could be used in almost any room in the house.

The life of some people in the major cities at that time was a life of affluence. These people lived and entertained on a large scale. Their houses were large. They needed furniture of large size—four-poster beds with canopies, grandfather's clocks, great breakfronts and highboys and secretary desks. Dining

Early American furniture designs have great dignity and grace. They are beautiful in line and light enough in scale to be appropriate in present-day homes.

tables of this period could seat sixteen people easily. Tables were sometimes designed to expand to seat twenty-four or thirty guests.

Adaptations. Today's manufacturers of furniture in the grand style of the eighteenth century have had to adapt it to the homes and life-styles of twentieth-century consumers. They have reduced the size of such furniture so that it fits our smaller houses and apartments. They have lowered the height of cabinets, breakfronts, and bedposts, to accommodate our lower ceilings. They have simplified the decoration to ease our housekeeping. But in the best reproductions and adaptations, the manufacturers have retained the beauty of line and detail that were characteristic of this golden period in furniture history.

Eighteenth-century furniture can be formal or informal in feeling. It looks best in settings that strive for a quiet, simple elegance.

Eighteenth-Century French Furniture

The elegant French furniture of the eighteenth century was quite different from that of England and the United States at the same time. French furniture of the cities went through three styles or changes, each elegant in its own way.

First came the style known as *Louis XV*. This featured light, delicate furniture that was fragile in appearance. The lines were graceful, and curved. The furniture of Louis XV was usually painted white or light colors, and its carving was decorated with gilding (highlighting with gold).

The next period, *Louis XVI*, was in many ways like the preceding period. The furniture had light, delicate lines. Surfaces were painted and gilded. But where Louis XV furniture was based on the curve, Louis XVI furniture was based on the straight line.

The third important style of French eighteenth-century furniture is *Directoire*. It was heavier than its two predecessors. Directoire was made of

---

Energy Tips

The winged chair, which originated in the eighteenth century, was designed to protect the body from chilly drafts and to cradle the warmth from a fireplace. High-backed upholstered furniture is still good protection against drafts.

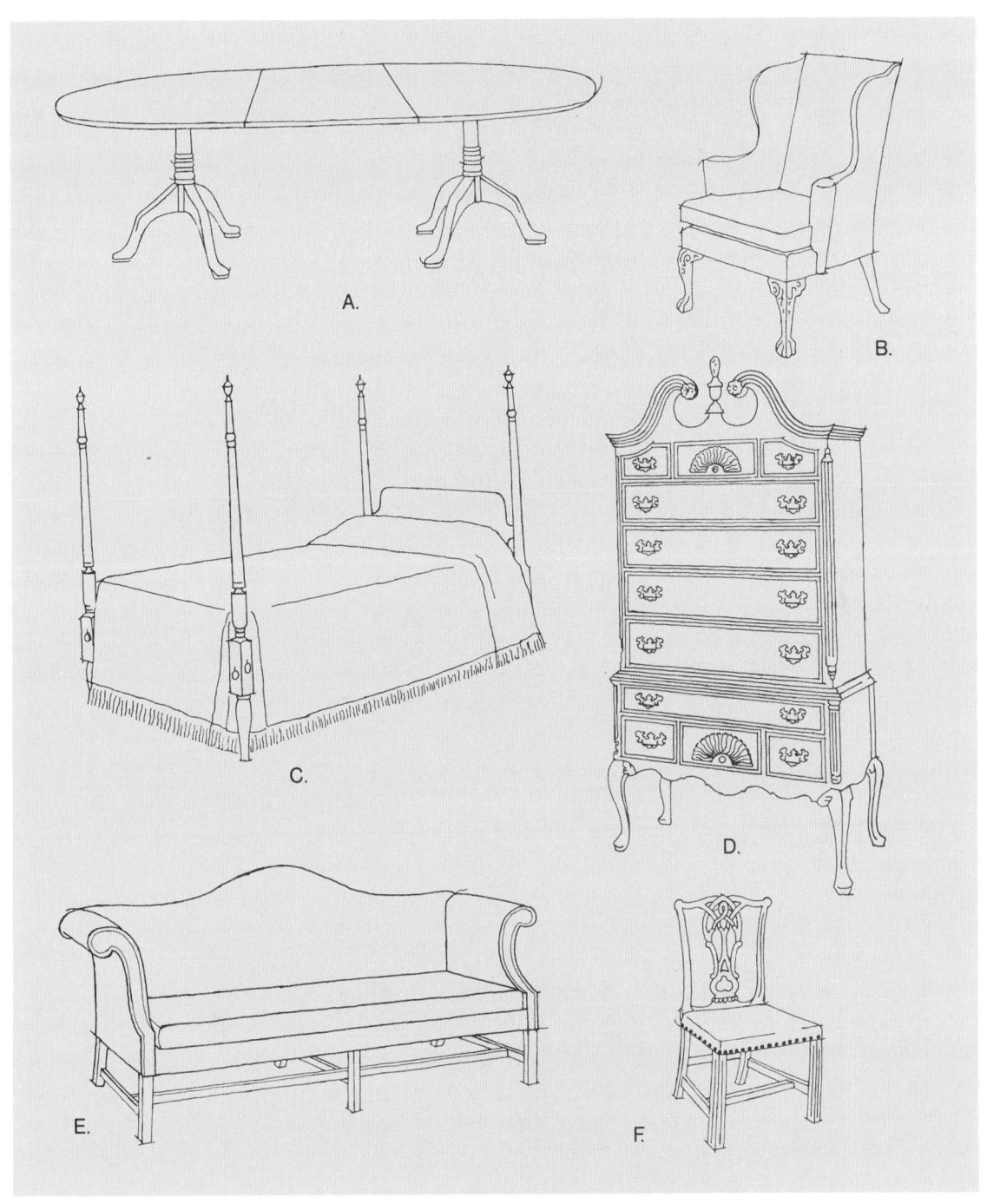

Eighteenth-century English and American furniture: (A) the double-pedestal dining table can be extended for extra space; (B) this wing chair features a claw-and-ball foot borrowed from Oriental furniture design; (C) the four-poster bed may support a canopy; (D) the swan-neck top of this highboy is a feature of Eighteenth-century design; (E) the camel's hump sofa is formal or casual, depending upon the upholstery; (F) the occasional chair was a contribution of Thomas Chippendale.

Victorian furniture: (A) Victorian sofas often lack the comfort and versatility required by modern homemakers; (B) the Victorian ladies' chair can be used as an accent piece in present-day rooms; (C) this chest is a simplified version of an ornate Victorian chest; (D) this headboard is an adaptation of the Victorian style; (E) the heavy pedestal base is an example of Victorian ornamentation; (F) the small-scale Victorian side chair provides ample seating.

mahogany, and decorated with brass. It was upholstered in leather, horsehair, and heavy silk. Directoire furniture had a simple, strong elegance.

Adaptations. Today's reproductions of these three furniture styles are, in many ways, quite faithful to the originals. All three styles are used to some extent today. But the Directoire style is the most popular of the three because of its greater strength of design. The daintiness of Louis XV and Louis XVI furniture tends to limit its use somewhat. Today, these pieces are used often in bedrooms. In living rooms, they are most effective with tapestries, oriental rugs, and crystal chandeliers.

Victorian Furniture

Nineteenth-century Victorian furniture reflected the taste of Queen Victoria, who ruled England for over 75 years. Many of the original pieces of this period are still in attics and antique shops today.

There was much that was beautiful about the early Victorian furniture. Its design has much in common with the beautiful curved-line furniture of the Louis XV style. Its decorative carving was restrained. Its upholstered chairs were comfortable for people of small stature, and the light scale of this furniture made it fit well into small rooms. The small sofas were graceful but some lacked comfort. The small, wood-backed chairs had great charm.

Used as Accents. Later Victorian furniture became massive and poorly designed. Line, proportion, and artistic restraint were disregarded.

Because of their availability, the antiques of the Victorian period are being used as accent pieces in many homes today. They are becoming more expensive as the supply dwindles, but you can still find a bargain. Original pieces and reproductions of this furniture are most effective when used with periodless upholstered furniture. Such furniture lends a feeling of contemporary comfort to a room, yet allows the Victorian furniture to dominate decoratively.

CONTEMPORARY FURNITURE

The contemporary, modern, or twentieth-century furniture styles grew out of a demand for something completely different from earlier styles. People

The beautiful French furniture styles of the eighteenth century were designed for French courts. This was Marie Antionette's room at Fontainebleau.

wanted furniture that would be expressive of this century. The first examples of modern furniture were exhibited at the Paris Exposition of 1925. Ever since then, many furniture designers have concentrated exclusively on developing furniture designs that express the essence of twentieth-century life as they saw it.

Historical Influences

It is impossible to pinpoint any single past style and say that it, more than any other, has influenced furniture design in this century. But much of the best of early twentieth-century design seems to owe a great deal to Oriental influence. For centuries, Oriental furniture has been characterized by simplicity. Oriental furniture emphasizes straight lines, undecorated surfaces, and smooth materials. All of these features are prominent in much contemporary furniture, too. At the same time, however, twentieth-century designs have also clearly been influenced by many other furniture styles. Styles from ancient Greece, the Italian Renaissance, and the Art Nouveau period in the 1890s have all made their mark on modern furniture.

A significant contribution to modern furniture was made by the Scandinavian countries during the 1940s and 1950s. Scandinavian designs are still popular. This furniture is generally made of light-colored woods. Beech, ash, and bleached oak are common materials. It is flowing, smooth, and light in design and scale. Its fabric coverings are often made of such "homey" materials as linen and cotton. These fabrics are frequently printed in bright colors and bold designs.

Contemporary furniture of the 1960s and 1970s made use of such industrial materials as chrome, glass, steel, and plastic.

"PERIODLESS" UPHOLSTERED FURNITURE

Much of the upholstered furniture on the market today can be called *periodless*. This furniture is not designed in a specific style or period of the past. Rather, it is designed to be neutral enough in shape so that it can be used with furniture of any period.

Four Styles

There are four styles of periodless sofas and chairs. The *Lawson style* has slim, straight lines. Lawson pieces offer maximum seating comfort in minimum space. The *Tuxedo style* is slimmer than the Lawson style and has arms that are the same height as the back. The *Club style,* also called the *Charles of London style,* features wide, flat-topped arms. In contrast to the Lawson and Tuxedo styles, the Club style has a rather heavy general appearance. This makes it especially suitable for larger rooms or rugged settings. The fourth type of periodless upholstered furniture is the armless kind. Armless pieces are especially useful in small rooms because they appear to take up less space than the other styles do. Armless furniture is available in both straight and curved lines. Modular units are included in this category.

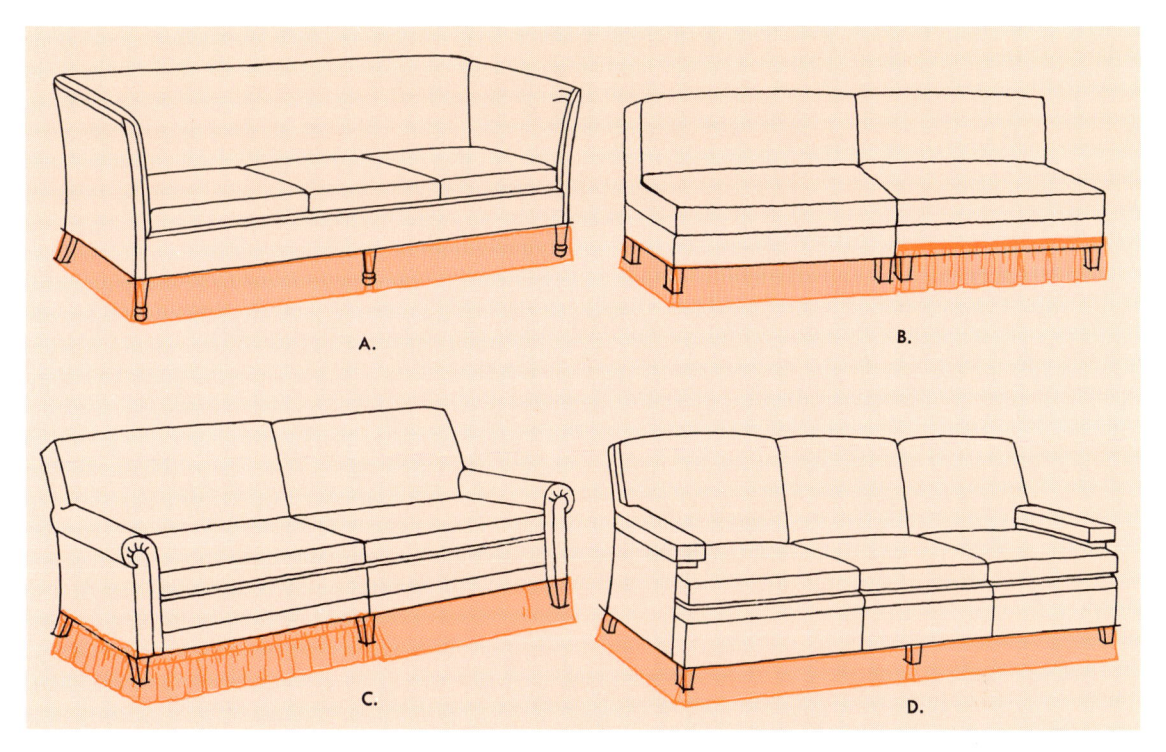

(A) the Tuxedo is a slim, dignified sofa that fits well in formal rooms. (B) the armless sofa is particularly usable in small rooms because of its slim lines. (C) the Lawson sofa, showing both formal and informal upholstery styles, illustrates the adaptability of periodless upholstered furniture. (D) the lines of the Club sofa give it a massive, heavy look.

SPACE-SAVING FURNITURE

Furniture with Double Functions

Some furniture is available now that does double duty in the home. Such furniture serves more than one function. For example, there are sofas, loveseats, and upholstered chairs that quickly and easily convert to beds. You simply remove their seat cushions and pull out the hidden spring and mattress. A *loftbed* is a *single bunk bed* with a seating or working area underneath.

You can also buy end tables that do double duty as filing cabinets. Some sewing machine cabinets also function as desks. You can also purchase nightstands, end tables, and bookcase bases that function as television cabinets. There are desk-dining table combination pieces, too.

Many pieces of furniture can be used for their surface area and their storage capability. For example, a footlocker or small trunk that serves as a coffee table or end table can be holding extra clothes and household items. A large rattan chest with a piece of glass cut to fit the top can do double duty, too. Wooden or plastic storage cubes can be topped with cushions for extra seating plus storage.

The important thing in choosing a double-duty piece of furniture is to be sure that it easily and conveniently serves both functions you want it to serve.

Furniture can be designed to conserve valuable space. Such furniture leaves the room free for a work spece of general activities. Would this type of bed, which is lowered from the ceiling, provide needed space in your home?

Folding Furniture

Some folding furniture is meant to always be part of the regular room furnishings. Other folding furniture is designed to be put away when it is not in use. Which type you choose will depend on how much storage space you have. For example, some folding chairs are neither comfortable enough nor attractive enough to use all the time. They are meant to be stored in a closet or under a bed and taken out only when there is an unusually large number of people to be seated. Other folding chairs, however, are both comfortable and attractive. Chairs such as these can be used as permanent furnishings.

Tables are available in a variety of folding styles, too. Some fold up completely and are meant to be stored. Others have drop-leaves that fold down to make the table smaller. With the leaves down, the table can stand against a wall, taking up little space. When needed, the table can be moved into the center of the room. Its leaves can then be raised to make it a large dining table.

Work or table surfaces that fold down from the wall can be constructed with finished wood and hinges.

Beds, too, can be of the folding variety. We have already mentioned beds that are folded up inside upholstered furniture. There are also roll-away beds, meant to be stored in a closet when not in use. There is another kind of folding bed that is designed to be attached to the inside of a closet door. When the closet door is open, the bed can be lowered down into the room. The simplest folding bed is the *bedroll,* or sleeping blanket. You may think such a bed is "for outdoors only." But a sleeping roll can be an excellent solution to the problem of how to accommodate the once-in-a-great-while overnight guest.

Modular Furniture

Yet another kind of space-saving furniture is called *modular* furniture. A manufacturer will design a large number of different pieces of furniture that all share the same basic dimensions. The basic set of dimensions is called a *module*. All of the components, or different elements, of a modular furniture system can be combined easily with one another. The parts are interchangeable, because

This modular group stands four-square in the middle of a living room. The combination of armless and corner sections plus ottomans is easily adapted to family rooms and bedrooms.

they share the same dimensions. Some modular systems use elements that can be stacked on top of one another. Other modular systems are designed to be fastened to the walls. Modular systems provide cabinets, chests, or drawers for closed storage of items and shelves for open display of items.

MONEY-SAVING FURNITURE

Do-It-Yourself Furniture

Lumber yards and hardware stores offer an increasingly large selection of materials for creating your own furniture. Well-planned do-it-yourself furniture can be attractive and reasonable in cost. Even if you are "all thumbs" when it comes to working with tools, you'll be surprised at the excellent results you can achieve on a do-it-yourself basis. Modern techniques and materials bring many do-it-yourself furniture projects within almost anyone's capabilities.

You can make a desk by using a 76-centimeter (30-inch) high bookshelf and a 76-centimeter (30-inch) high filing cabinet as base supports. On top of these supports, place a flush door (a door with no panels) or a piece of cut-to-size plywood. The door or the piece of plywood serves as the desk top.

To create a studio bed, buy six screw-on furniture legs. Attach the legs to a piece of plywood cut to the same size as your spring and mattress. Place the spring and mattress on the plywood base to finish your bed.

To convert your studio bed into a sofa, hang a large curtain pole to the wall above the bed's long side. From the pole, hang bolsters or cushions to which you've attached large fabric loops.

There are many other do-it-yourself furniture projects that you can attempt. Magazines that cover the subject of home decoration will provide you with many ideas for projects. You can also check your library for books on the subject.

Remodeling Furniture

Secondhand furniture is often available at little or no cost. Relatives may offer you pieces they are no longer using. You may find some pieces at yard sales, rummage sales, and in secondhand shops. Such furniture often has many

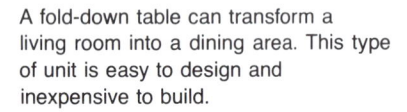

A fold-down table can transform a living room into a dining area. This type of unit is easy to design and inexpensive to build.

Secondhand furniture can be an economical and practical design solution. Notice how this old trunk makes an attractive window seat.

superficial defects; that is, problems that make the piece look worse than it really is. But with a little imagination and hard work, you can often convert somebody else's throw-away into a unique and beautiful piece of furniture.

Much old furniture needs to be refinished before it looks good enough to put back into use. A good sanding and painting are often all it takes to make a piece attractive.

Unfinished Furniture

A wide variety of furniture pieces in a wide variety of styles is now available in unfinished condition. The wood such pieces are made of is usually soft, and the quality of construction is often poor. However, if you don't plan to keep unfinished pieces a lifetime, they can be a wise choice. You should try to avoid buying unfinished pieces with drawers or doors, however. Drawers and doors on these pieces almost inevitably warp in time. This warping makes the furniture both unsightly and unusable.

Probably the best way to finish unfinished furniture is to paint it. But it can also be stained effectively. There are also "antiquing" kits available today. These are furniture refinishing kits designed for use with both old and new furniture. Antiquing with these kits is a three-step process. The result is an interestingly textured and colored finish. Or, if you like the look of natural wood, simply apply a coat of varnish or wax.

Outdoor Furniture

Yet another source of inexpensive furniture is the department of your local furniture store that specializes in outdoor or patio furniture. This furniture is designed to be used primarily in casual, out-of-door settings. Some pieces are made of rattan, straw, or wicker. Such pieces are usually comfortable but not particularly long-lasting. Other outdoor furniture is made of canvas, metal, or plastic. These pieces are likely to be both comfortable and durable.

COMBINING FURNITURE

One of the most difficult interior-design questions to answer is: "Will this go with that?" You may be considering a half-dozen individual pieces of furniture, each of which is beautiful and useful in itself. But can you combine all the pieces harmoniously? Will they create the mood and feeling you want?

The answer is: look for harmonies or the same qualities among the various pieces of furniture you are considering.

Wood Tone. Look for harmony of wood tones. Furniture in a room should not necessarily match, but it should blend. Is most of the wood in the furniture you have chosen more or less the same color? If so, you have found a harmony. An occasional accent piece in a completely different color will sometimes enhance a room, of course. But for pleasing harmony, most of the furniture pieces should be similar in their wood tones.

Mood. Look for harmony of mood. Are most of the pieces of furniture formal in mood? Or are they informal? Are most of them rough and crude? Or are most of them elegant and highly polished? If you choose your pieces for harmony of mood, that will help ensure that they all "go together."

Line. Look for harmony of line. Are most of the pieces gracefully curved? Are most of them straight? Are they delicate or solid and substantial?

Scale. Also look for harmony of scale. Are most of the pieces small in size, with low backs and narrow profiles? Or are the pieces large, with solid profiles?

Other harmonies to consider are harmony of surface treatments; harmony of color values; and harmony of textures. The more harmonies you strive for in selecting your pieces, the surer you can be that they will work together attractively. When you have established the harmonies, you can choose a few special pieces of furniture or accessories for a splash of color contrast. A bit of contrast highlights a harmonious room.

Unfinished furniture has become very popular in recent years. It comes in a wide variety of pieces and in several styles. Since unfinished furniture tends to be made of soft wood, the quality of the construction must be carefully evaluated.

Careers

An antique dealer, usually self-employed, knows the sources and authenticity of goods he or she sells. Often, the sources are well-guarded secrets in this competitive field. Most dealers specialize in one type of antiques, whether it is early American or Chinese.

An antique dealer is, in a sense, an historian. He or she looks for signatures on handmade crafts and can identify the type of material on the inside and outside. The styles of the past and of early craftspersons must be as familiar as those of modern day. It takes a great deal of knowledge about history and geography to identify silverware, furniture, and other goods for their authenticity.

College is not necessary but may be helpful. Preparing for a career in antiques may take many years of retail sales, as well as visits to museums, rural towns, auctions, and a great deal of travel. One must read a vast amount and talk to people in the antique business. Good decision-making skills are necessary. The dealer must make good and often quick judgments on whether to purchase an item, how to price it, and how to predict market demands.

Learning Experiences

1. Choose one of the famous cabinetmakers listed below and prepare a research report on the style of furniture associated with that cabinetmaker:

Sheraton	Chippendale	Phyfe
Belter	Adam	Hitchcock
Biedermeier	Eames	

2. As a class, check home magazines to find the names of furniture companies and send for their catalogs so you can see what is currently available.

3. Explore secondhand stores and antique shops to see what used furniture is available and what it costs. Compare these prices with those of new furniture shown in shops or catalogs.

4. Design a piece of furniture for your own use. Draw or describe it for the class.

5. Prepare a bulletin-board display of pictures of chairs. Use as many different types of chair designs as you can find from as many different historical periods as possible. Arrange the photographs in chronological order. Under them, draw a time line.

CHAPTER 5

Buying Furniture

The whole process of buying furniture is an extremely personal one. Nobody else can tell you what you should buy. Nor can anyone tell you what will best meet your needs. Other people can make suggestions, of course, and suggestions should be listened to with an open mind. But ultimately, the decision must be yours. You must analyze your own situation carefully, thoughtfully, and objectively to ensure that the furniture you choose will be right for you.

Know Your Functional Needs

Furniture is necessary because it helps you do the things you want to do comfortably and conveniently. A beautiful piece of furniture is of little useful value if it does not serve a function. Any furniture-buying plan must begin, then, with an understanding of the functions you want your furniture to perform.

If the room for which you are buying furniture is your bedroom, ask yourself: In what ways do I intend to use this room? If you study in your bedroom, you may need a desk and a strong reading lamp. Do you entertain friends there? If so, comfortable seating will be important. Think over your needs carefully and make a list of the furniture pieces you will need.

Know Your Personality

Is good quality important to you? Would you rather have one fine thing than twenty cheap ones? If so, your furniture-buying plan will probably involve making only an occasional purchase. That means you will have to decide which single piece of furniture is most important to acquire first. Later, when you can afford another major investment, you will decide what your next purchase should be.

Is change important to you? Many people become restless without fairly frequent changes in their surroundings. If you are one of these people, you may

This modular furniture system is flexible and easy to live with. The back and seat cushions are connected with pine battens.

have to sacrifice some quality in the furniture you buy to ensure that you can afford to change that furniture with some degree of frequency. You may also decide to look for furniture that can be readily changed in appearance rather than replaced. Upholstered pieces with simple lines would be a good choice. Such pieces can be slipcovered easily. Wooden furniture with a minimum of or no carving or other decoration will prove easier to refinish than ornate styles.

Know Your Physical Needs

Everyone has individual physical qualities. These qualities help determine what furniture will be comfortable. Your height, for example, has an effect on the kinds of seating that are right for you. Deep seats with high backs are necessary for tall people. Short people, on the other hand, can be quite uncomfortable in a deep-seated chair or sofa. As a general rule, if both tall and short people will be using the furniture, it is best to choose upholstered chairs and sofas that will accommodate the shorter members of the household. Taller people can sit on an angle and make themselves comfortable.

What about your weight? Heavy people require firmer upholstery to be comfortable. They also are more comfortable in sturdy-looking furniture. A delicate-looking chair may, in fact, be very strong, but heavy people are likely to feel psychological discomfort when sitting in such a chair.

What about allergies? If you suffer from allergies, you may need to choose upholstered furniture containing only synthetic materials in its filling. Do you

---

Energy Tips

Soft fabric gives a warmer feeling than leather, plastic, or wood does. A warm-colored slipcover or throw cover made of soft, fuzzy fabric seems to add a layer of warmth to furniture.

have a bad back? If so, you will probably need a hard mattress for your bed. You will also need chairs that allow you to sit up straight.

Know Your Budget Limitations

We may wish we had unlimited money for designing or redecorating a room. But none of us has unlimited resources. So, it is important to realistically determine how much you can afford to spend on furniture.

The Unit System

Once you know what furniture you need and what your budget limitations are, turn to the chart on page 300. This shows a furnishings budget on a unit basis. The chart contains information about comparative costs of furniture that you will find helpful.

Tradeoffs

Of course, the chart is useful only as a starting point. You cannot rely on it completely. You may not be planning to purchase every item shown on the chart. A good buy on one furniture item will mean that you will have more to spend on another. If you decide to slipcover a chair you now own, you may save some money for a new chair you still need. After considering your needs and your budget, you may decide to do some "trading off." For example, you might select large floor pillows to provide seating if you cannot afford the loveseat you had at first hoped to purchase.

But though it cannot serve as the ultimate budgeting tool, the unit system of planning your furnishing budget can provide helpful guidelines. And remember, an estimate of your initial furniture costs is just that—*an estimate*. Estimates can help you plan your purchases. But you will have to make adjustments in your budget once you determine the actual costs of the items you plan to buy.

The quality of upholstered furniture is judged by the details of the stitching and by the firmness and the comfort of the padding and springs.

EVALUATING FURNITURE ACCORDING TO QUALITY

Many people decide whether or not a piece of furniture is of good quality by looking at its price tag. These people assume that the more expensive the piece is, the better its quality must be. Obviously, there is often a relationship between quality and price. To be sure whether or not a piece of furniture is well made, look at furniture itself, not at its price tag.

Wood Furniture

There are many myths about the quality of wood furniture: "Maple furniture is cheap." "Mahogany furniture is expensive." "Solid wood is a sign of quality." "Veneered wood is a sign of cheap construction." Each of these statements *may* be true when applied to a particular piece of furniture. But none of them is true when applied to furniture in general.

Wood used in furniture may be either hardwood or softwood. Hardwood generally comes from trees that have broad, flat leaves that drop in the autumn. Birch, oak, maple, cherry, walnut, and mahogany are all hardwoods. Softwoods, on the other hand, generally come from evergreen trees. Red cedar, fir, white pine, and spruce are common softwoods. There are exceptions, however. Basswood, for example, is a softwood, though it comes from a tree that sheds its leaves. Cypress is a hardwood, though it comes from an evergreen.

Hardwoods. Hardwoods are excellent materials for furniture. They all take a good finish; that is, they can all be sanded and polished to give their surfaces a rich, smooth appearance. Most hardwoods have an attractive *grain* (natural lines in the wood itself that form a subtle pattern). Another advantage of hardwoods in furniture making is that their cell structure allows them to hold glue and screws securely.

In evaluating chests and dressers, check for dovetailed joints and for center guides on the bottom of drawers to make them pull straight.

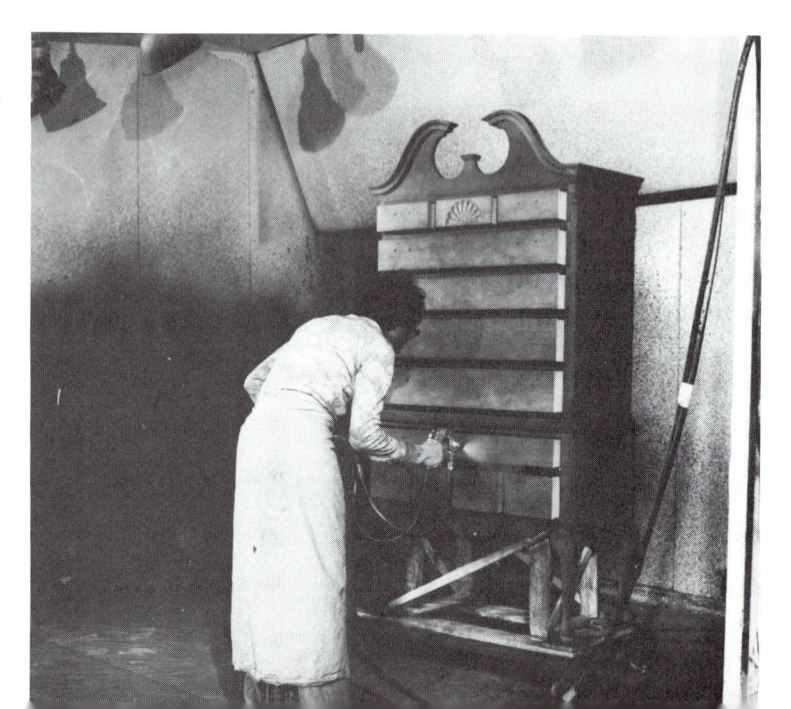

Softwoods. Softwoods are generally less expensive than hardwoods. This is because evergreen trees grow at a much faster rate than *deciduous* (leaf-dropping) trees. So softwood supplies are constantly being replenished. Inexpensive furniture, such as unfinished furniture or rustic patio furniture, is usually made of softwood. Softwood splits and splinters more easily than hardwood does. Therefore, it does not hold screws as well as hardwood. Softwood also dents easily. This means that you must be careful not to treat softwood furniture harshly. On the other hand, softwood has a more conspicuous grain than hardwood. This type of grain gives softwoods a strong textural interest.

Solid Wood. Furniture made of solid wood is of good quality only if the wood has been carefully selected and processed. The term *solid wood* means that the same wood board visible on the outside of the furniture continues all the way through to the inside surface. If the manufacturer used poor wood or failed to dry the wood properly, solid wood may warp and crack in such a way that the piece can never be repaired.

Veneered Wood. The use of veneered wood in furniture construction is neither modern nor necessarily inexpensive. A veneer is a thin sheet of expensive, often exotic, wood such as walnut, zebrawood, or rosewood. A veneer sheet is glued over the surface of less-expensive wood. Mahogany veneer, for example, can give a piece of furniture the look of solid mahogany. But, in fact, only the surface of the piece is covered with mahogany. The base, or *core*, may be spruce or birch. Using veneers makes it possible to bring exotic woods into a moderate price range. It also makes possible the matching of wood grains. For example, veneers can be used on cabinet doors to give them identical natural wood surfaces. When veneers are applied to large surfaces, they also help prevent warping. But poorly constructed veneer can cause problems of its own. Such veneer may separate from the wood to which it was glued. Veneer also is usually harder to refinish than solid wood. If you are considering an old piece of furniture, look carefully at the top edge of a door or drawer. It will be easy to see whether the piece is solid wood or veneered.

Looking at Construction. Ultimately, quality of wood depends upon the integrity of the manufacturer. Industry regulations require new furniture to be clearly tagged with information about the materials used. Study such tags carefully when you are choosing wood furniture pieces.

In addition to the wood itself, the quality of a piece of wood furniture depends upon the quality of its construction. If a piece of furniture is well constructed, its legs will remain solid. The drawers will slide easily, and the doors will fit. There are certain construction details that ensure these results, and you can check them.

Fastenings. The chief thing to look for is the way in which parts of the piece of furniture have been fastened to each other. Staples or nails and glue are usually used in the construction of poor-quality furniture. Wood screws usually indicate a better quality of construction. *Corner blocks* (triangular blocks of wood tucked into and fastened to the right angle where two pieces of wood join) are a sign of quality construction. So is the use of reinforcing *dowels* (circular wooden rods inserted into adjoining pieces of wood to help hold them tightly together). The round edges of the dowels will be clearly visible on furniture reinforced by this method.

Joints. The kinds of joints used on a piece of furniture are also an indication of its relative quality. *Butt joints* indicate poor quality. In a butt joint, the edges of two pieces of wood are simply lined up next to each other. *Dovetailed joints* are a superior type of joint. In this style of joinery, the edges of two pieces of wood are cut in a pattern of wedge-shaped notches. The wedges (shaped like the tails of doves) on one piece fit into and interlock with the gaps in the other. *Rabbet joints* are simpler versions of dovetails with just a single cut in each piece of wood lining up with and interlocking with a cut in its neighbor. Rabbet joints are not as strong as dovetailed joints, but they are superior to butt joints.

Center Guides. In evaluating cabinets, chests, and dressers, check for *center guides* on the bottom of the drawers. Such guides help the drawers pull out straight and slide back easily. They indicate quality construction. Inferior pieces containing drawers have an open space between the bottom of the drawer and the contents of the drawer below it. Better quality pieces have thin, shelflike pieces of wood inserted under every drawer. You can check for this feature by removing one of the drawers of the piece. Even when the drawer is removed, you cannot see directly into the drawer below. You should also check to see whether the piece stands level on the floor or whether it rocks a bit. If the piece has doors, check to be sure they open and close easily. Doors should also stay closed as they are supposed to and should meet correctly at the center of the piece. Another thing to inspect is the hardware (hinges, knobs, pulls) on the piece. Is the hardware securely fastened?

Finish. Judging the quality of the *finish* (the surface treatment) of wood furniture is a bit more difficult than evaluating construction. Certainly, you

Antique furniture often shows careful attention to details of construction. Contemporary reproductions, such as this buffet, often use the same methods.

The wedge-shaped notches of this drawer are the dovetail joinings, an indication of quality construction.

SIGNS OF GOOD FURNITURE CONSTRUCTION

Guide Strips

A.

B.

Dovetail joining

C.

Doweled joint

D.

E.

FACE VENEER
CROSS BAND
CORE
CROSS BAND
BACK VENEER

F.

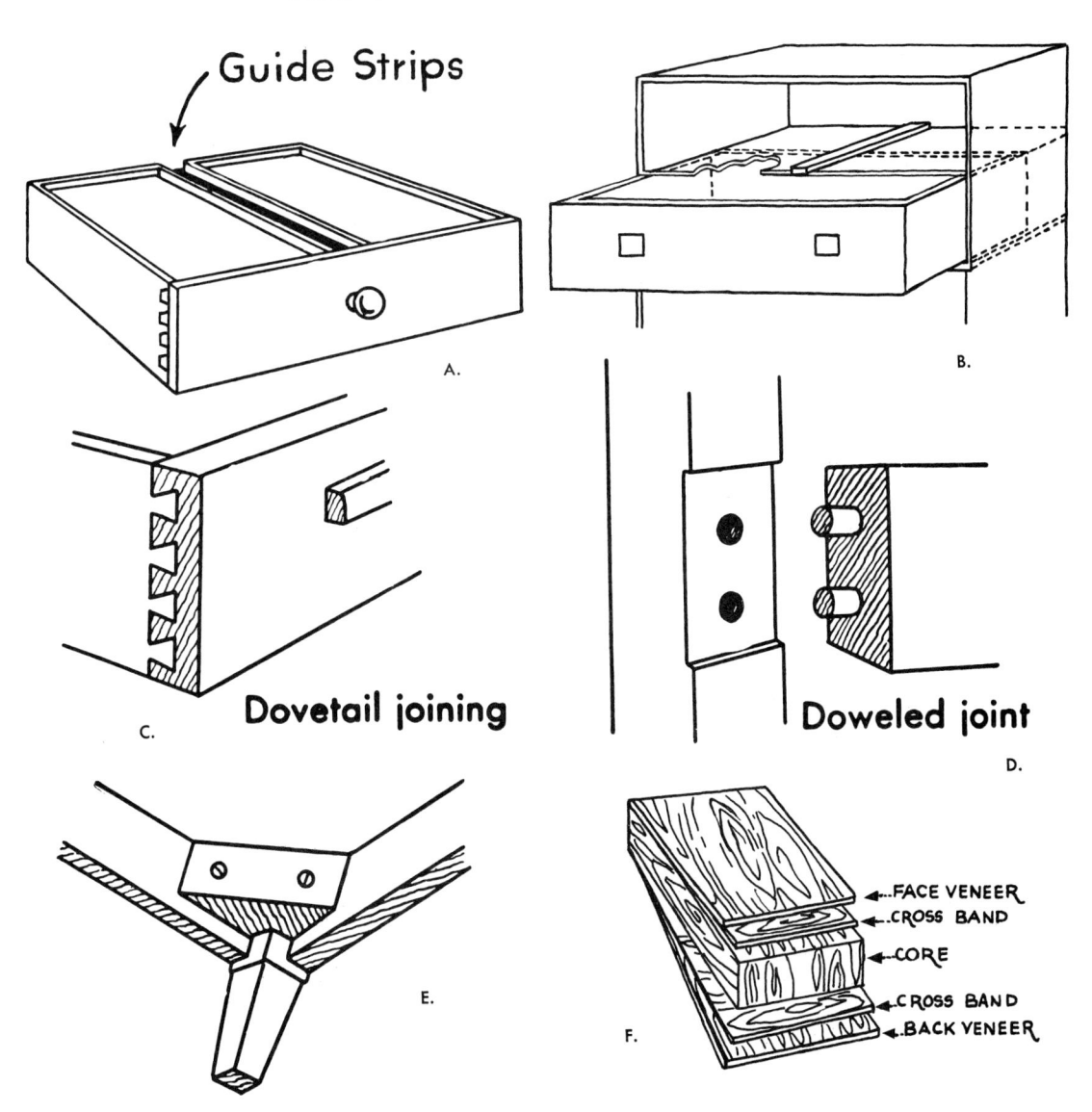

Screwed-in corner block

(A) Center glides on the bottom of drawers keeps them sliding in and out evenly. (B) Dustproof construction—a wooden shelf to which the second part of the center glide is attached—is another mark of quality. (C) Dovetail joining is the mark of good construction on drawers. (D) Doweled joints help to ensure continuing strength and rigidity. (E) Screwed-in corner blocking is another means of producing solid construction. (F) Veneer wood consists of a center core plus thin sheets of plywood with the grain running in opposite directions.

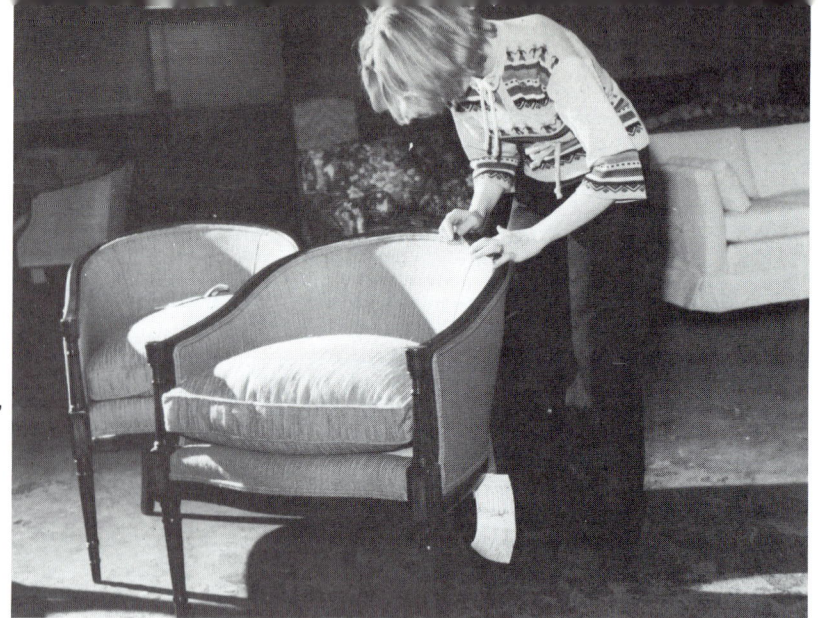

Shopping for upholstered furniture is a special skill because the upholstery methods, the inside materials, and the frame construction are completely covered. The exposed wood finish, the upholstery fabric, the tailoring, and the labels which identify the filling materials are the indications of the total quality.

should run your hand along the top and sides of the piece to be sure that it is completely smooth. A well-made piece of *case furniture* (furniture that has drawers or doors or shelves) will have no rough, unsanded wood used anywhere in its construction.

Some new furniture is manufactured with a heat-resistant finish. Wood tops of such pieces as dining tables, coffee tables, bars, television cabinets, and the like have been *impregnated* (filled) or covered with a plastic substance. The plastic helps those surfaces withstand damage from water, alcohol, cigarette burns, and other careless use. For some rooms, furniture with such finishes can be an excellent choice. Occasionally, these finishes make a piece look hard and artificial. For that reason, heat-resistant finishes may be inappropriate in rooms where a soft, warm mood is desired. Another drawback to pieces finished this way is that they cannot easily be refinished if they are damaged or if you wish to change their appearance.

Upholstered Furniture

Judging the quality of a piece that has been completely upholstered is difficult. The construction of the frame, the upholstery methods used, and the material used for inner padding are all hidden from view. If any wood surfaces are visible, study them. Also evaluate the quality of the upholstery fabric and the quality of the *tailoring* (sewing). Finally, check the label that identifies the filling material used inside the piece.

Fabric and Tailoring. To check the quality of the fabric and the tailoring, study the piece closely. Does the fabric look as though it will stand up to long, hard wear, or does it look flimsy and thin? Is it likely to catch and pull easily? Has the stitching been carefully done? If the piece has pleats, are they tightly sewed and evenly spaced? Is the same true of any buttons attached to the piece? Is the *welting* (the three-dimensional binding) sewed tightly and evenly? Run your hand across the complete surface of each pillow in the seat and back. Does the piece seem smoothly filled, or are there bumps and ridges?

Inner Construction. As far as the inner construction of the piece is concerned, you are completely dependent on the integrity of the manufacturer and of the retailer who is selling the piece. For this reason, choose a store carefully when you are considering the purchase of an upholstered piece.

Comfort. A final thing to check before you buy an upholstered piece is sitting comfort. If the piece is hard and uncomfortable, do not consider the piece further. It will not improve with age or use. If the piece is soft and luxurious, yet inexpensive, be careful. Such pieces are often of poor quality and will not stand up to long use. A piece that is firm and yet comfortable, with a price comparable to the prices of other similar upholstered pieces, is probably well constructed. But again, the reputations of the retailer and the manufacturer are the most important factors in ensuring that the piece will wear well.

SHOPPING PROCEDURES

Decide When You Will Buy

By timing your furniture purchases, you can save money and avoid disappointment. February and August are the months for major clearance sales at most large, reputable furniture dealers. Special sales can, of course, be held at any time. Usually, the store personnel know in advance when a sale will occur.

Furniture is only seldom available for immediate delivery. If you buy a piece "right off the floor," it can be delivered right away. But most of the time, new furniture has to be ordered. Delivery takes anywhere from two weeks to three months. If you "special order" (that is, request a fabric or finish that is not regularly stocked at the warehouse), you may have to wait even longer. Try to have the store give you a firm delivery date when you make your purchase.

Decide Where You Will Buy

Wholesale Showrooms. Wholesale furniture showrooms are open to many people. Some showrooms have a policy of opening to the public. At other showrooms, admittance is by invitation only. Open invitations are given to interior designers and their clients. Wholesale suppliers frequently have far more furniture for shoppers to choose from than retail outlets. Another advantage is economic. You can save money on your purchases if the wholesaler is indeed selling at wholesale prices. However, it is essential that you do some comparison shopping to be sure that the wholesaler's price is truly a bargain. Also, remember to consider any extra costs resulting from buying from a wholesale outlet (such as delivery charges, showroom charges, or furniture set-up charges). These charges might already be built into the price at a retail outlet.

Retail Stores. Retail furniture stores do offer the advantage of providing a

Today, tag sales and community-sponsored rummage sales have become a popular way to shop for furniture. Often, imaginative and economical furnishings are found. Can you think of any drawbacks connected with this type of buying?

variety of services to customers. A retail store is more likely than a wholesale store to let you pay repeated visits to look around while you are making up your mind. A retail store is likely to provide you with swatches of fabric to take home and study. But there is no question that retail stores charge enough for each piece of furniture to ensure themselves of a healthy profit. So, retail prices are often not as attractive as prices at other furniture sources. Watch for the sales at retail stores. You can sometimes get a good buy on a floor sample that is not too shopworn.

Catalog Houses. If you live outside a metropolitan area, an important source of furniture can be the "catalog" house. To use this source, you choose the item you want from a catalog. Then you place your order. Your order will be filled from a warehouse that handles orders from all over the country. Catalog houses buy furniture in tremendous quantity. Therefore, they can offer standard furniture items at surprisingly low prices. (When comparing costs, however, be sure to consider cost of shipping.)

There are two main disadvantages to shopping for furniture through a catalog house. One is that catalog suppliers tend to offer only "middle-of-the-road" styles of furniture. This is because their success depends on appealing to large numbers of people from many backgrounds. So, you are unlikely to find the unique or exotic special items in a catalog. The second disadvantage is that you cannot inspect the furniture before you order. You take quality on faith.

Salvage Stores. In many areas, it is possible to shop at large-discount railway- and-trucking salvage houses. Such stores offer almost no customer services. Usually, sales are final with no return of merchandise allowed. Many times, the furniture offered is flawed or damaged. You must buy it at your own risk. If, however, you find an item that you need and like, it is possible to save substantial sums of money at these salvage stores.

Antique and Secondhand Stores. Another source of furniture is the antique and secondhand furniture outlets. Most communities have several outlets for used furniture—including individual tag sales, yard sales, and garage sales. Other outlets may also be available, such as annual auctions and rummage sales sponsored by churches and community organizations. All of these offer distinct possibilities for the bargain hunter in need of furniture.

Plan Your Shopping Trip

A *buying* trip is the trip you take when you are actually ready to make your purchases. A *shopping* trip, on the other hand, involves obtaining information, comparing prices, and weighing alternative choices. Successful shopping trips must be carefully planned.

Information Needed. First, assemble the information you will need. Know which pieces of furniture you are looking for. Know your budget limitations. Take color samples along with you to the stores. Also bring floorplans with all the necessary room dimensions. If you are shopping for furniture, be sure to include on your list of dimensions any narrow opening through which large furniture pieces will have to be carried.

Time. Second, choose the time of your shopping trip carefully. Try to choose a time when salespeople will not be rushed or too tired. It is usually best to go early in the day, preferably on a day when most people are at work. Try not to go on days when the store is having a special sale. Then, choose your sales clerk carefully: do not let the sales clerk select *you!* If a sales clerk approaches you, simply ask if you can look around on your own. Then observe the different salespeople, and choose the one who treats customers the way you want to be treated. Ask that person to wait on you when he or she is free. When you are waited on, present all your information. If you give complete information about size, color, style, and price range, you will save time for yourself and the sales clerk. This will also win you respect and cooperation. Never hesitate to ask questions. Be sure to take notes. Ask about special ordering of upholstered pieces. Examine manufacturers' upholstery swatches. Ask about storing furniture. If you are not ready to have the furniture delivered at the time you buy, ask what arrangements can be made for storing it. Also ask about delivery costs. *Write the answers down.*

Selecting a salesperson who works well with you is important if you are going to enjoy and profit from the transaction.

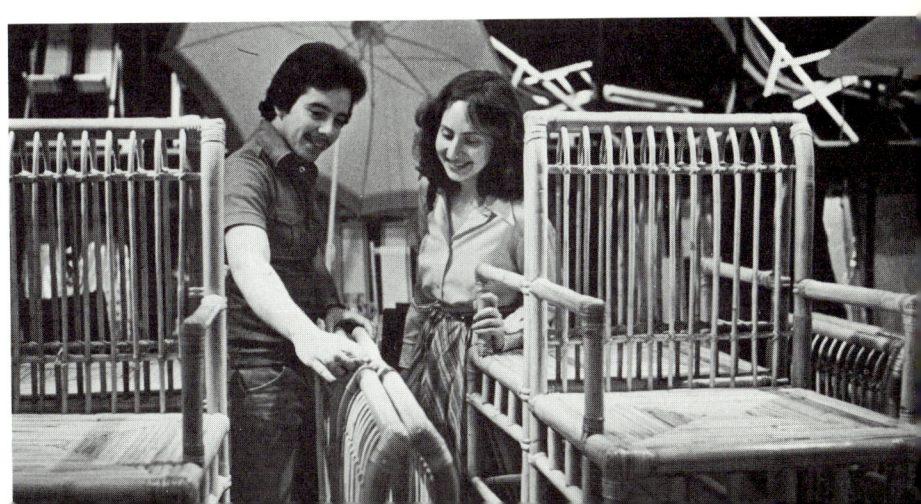

If decorator service is offered by the store you have chosen, use it. It costs you nothing. Often, it can help you make wise, attractive choices.

Paying for Your Purchase

If you pay with cash or a check, you do not have to consider credit arrangements. Almost all plans involving credit for longer than thirty days add to the cost of your purchase. Major credit cards allow you to spread out payments, and individual stores often have payment plans. Find out what interest rates are charged on these plans. Then figure how much the interest charges add to the price.

To use the Unit System: (a) deduct all units already obtained or not desired from number of units to be bought; (b) list remaining total number of units to be bought; (c) list total budget for furnishings; and (d) divide (c) by (b) for budget allowance for each unit. (Leon Pescheret's Estimate of Proportions and Costs of Furniture)

FURNISHING BUDGET ON THE UNIT SYSTEM

Three-room Apartment	Relative Unit Value	Number of Units in Apartment
Living room and dining room:		
Bookcase (unfinished)	1½	1½
Curtains (2 windows)	½ (each)	1
Easy chair (2)	1 (each)	2
Large table	2	2
Rug	1	1
Side chairs (3)	½ (each)	1½
Small table (unfinished)	¼	¼
Sofa	3	3
Total units		12¼
Bedroom:		
Chest (unfinished)	1½	1½
Curtains (2 windows)	½ (each)	1
Double bed	1	1
Mattress, spring, pillows	1½	1½
Mirror	¾	¾
Rugs	¾	¾
Side chair (unfinished)	¼	¼
Total units		6¾
Kitchen:		
Glass and china	1	1
Kitchen equipment	1	1
Linen (complete apartment)	1	1
Total units		3
Accessories:		
Blankets	1	1
Lamps (2)	¼ (each)	½
Pillows (2)	¼ (each)	½
Vases and pictures	1	1
		3

Finally, remember to take your time when buying. Never jump at a purchase. Take time to think about it and to comparison shop in other stores. Remember, it is *your* room you are furnishing—and *your* money you are spending.

SPECIAL DANGERS IN BUYING FURNITURE

Furniture can be bought in all price ranges. But it is safe to say that the most extravagantly advertised furniture has the least quality per dollar of cost. Such terms as "Gigantic savings!"; "Low, low, one-day sale ONLY"; and "Spectacular going-out-of-business sale" should make you cautious. As a rule, stores that use such terms are unloading furniture that careful shoppers would not want.

"Rooms full of furniture!" is another favorite advertising claim used by low-grade furniture outlets. A lamp or two and several small end tables are the bait that is dangled in front of your eyes to make you forget the poor quality or ugly design of the main pieces. But remember that nobody can afford to give away good merchandise. Something has to be wrong if the price is "ridiculously" low.

This does not mean that you should not buy when furniture is legitimately on sale. Quality-furniture shops have regular sales of fine-grade furniture. You can buy furniture at these sales that will give you good service. You can also save a great deal of money. But before you snap up a furniture bargain, be sure that it is *truly* a bargain. Merchandise flawed by poor workmanship or ugly design is never a bargain, no matter how low the cost.

Careers
There are many careers in the furniture industry. Business experience is sometimes more important than a college education in these jobs.

You might work in a large furniture store which has many departments and opportunities. A *merchandiser*, often with the owner, selects the goods that will sell. Highly trained *sales personnel* help customers select room arrangements and provide for credit. A *manager* supervises the sales and analyzes how the stock is moving. A person in the promotion department might arrange the showroom displays and handle store advertising.

Other career opportunities exist in wholesaling. In a warehouse, a *shipping clerk* takes responsibility for the inventory of goods. He or she receives shipments from the factory and arranges for deliveries to customers. *Business managers*, in addition to *truckers* and *clerks*, work here.

Perhaps you prefer to work with your hands or to be your own boss. *Carpenters* and *craftspeople* are always in demand to create custom-made furnishings. *Furniture finishers* specialize in decorating or antiquing and adding protective covering to unfinished furniture. *Upholsterers* often work in their own small shops to recover furniture for local clients. All of these skills can be learned during a person's high school years for use later as a vocation or a hobby.

Learning Experiences

1. Visit a large furniture showroom and examine a number of dressers in different price ranges. Make detailed notes about a very inexpensive example, a moderately priced example, and an expensive example. What differences in materials, construction details, and workmanship explain the difference in price? Describe circumstances under which each might be an appropriate choice.
2. Imagine that you are in the market for living-room furniture. Make a list of things for which you would look in shopping for such a major furniture purchase. Then, compare your list of points with those of your classmates. Are there items on other lists that you did not include on your list? Are there items that others have included that you think are unimportant? Why?
3. Collect small samples of various types of wood at a lumber yard. Mark each piece as to type of wood. Stain and finish each piece using the same stain and finishing method. What are the differences in the finished products? Try the experiment again using identical pieces of wood with different stains and finishes.
4. Imagine that you are going to shop for an upholstered chair for your family's living room. Interview each family member about what he or she thinks is important to look for when shopping. Arrange these points in a list of your own ranging from "most important quality to look for" to "least important quality."
5. Using the classified telephone directory, do a survey of types of stores in your community that sell furniture. How do these stores differ in price range, variety of choice, special services, and method of payment?

CHAPTER 6

Arranging Furniture

How beautiful a room looks, how comfortable it is, and how easily and conveniently it lends itself to the uses it was meant to serve depend not only on the furniture chosen, but on the way that furniture is arranged. Furniture that is put "just any old place" in a room not only looks uninviting but also prevents the room from being used as fully and as comfortably as it should be. For example, you may tuck an easy chair into a corner of your living room all by itself. But you will find that people quickly stop choosing to sit in that chair if it does not have a nearby lamp to make reading comfortable. The chair will also be less useful if it does not have a table next to it so that people have a place to set down a coffee cup or a magazine. Also, in the corner, the chair may be too far from the other seating pieces, so that the eye-contact necessary to conversation is impossible to establish. That easy chair may be the most comfortable chair in the house. But poor furniture arrangement can make it an all-but-useless piece of furniture.

Mastering the skill of furniture arranging is not difficult once you have learned a few basic principles. This chapter will discuss those principles. It will also suggest how you can translate the principles into your own furniture arrangement plans.

START WITH A FLOORPLAN

One way to tell whether a piano would look better on one side of the living room than another is to move it and see. But after you have moved the piano once or twice, *and* the sofa, *and* the easy chair, *and* the television set, you will quickly come to the conclusion that there has to be a better way of trying out different furniture arrangements than hauling the furniture around. And you will be right.

Most interior designers perform the trial-and-error process of considering several different furniture arrangements by using a *floorplan*. A floorplan is a sort of map of the room. It is drawn from the point of view of someone looking at the entire room from above. The floorplan shows the shape of the room in outline. The plan shows such architectural features as doors, windows, and fireplaces, as well as such fixtures as electrical outlets and permanently attached wall lamps.

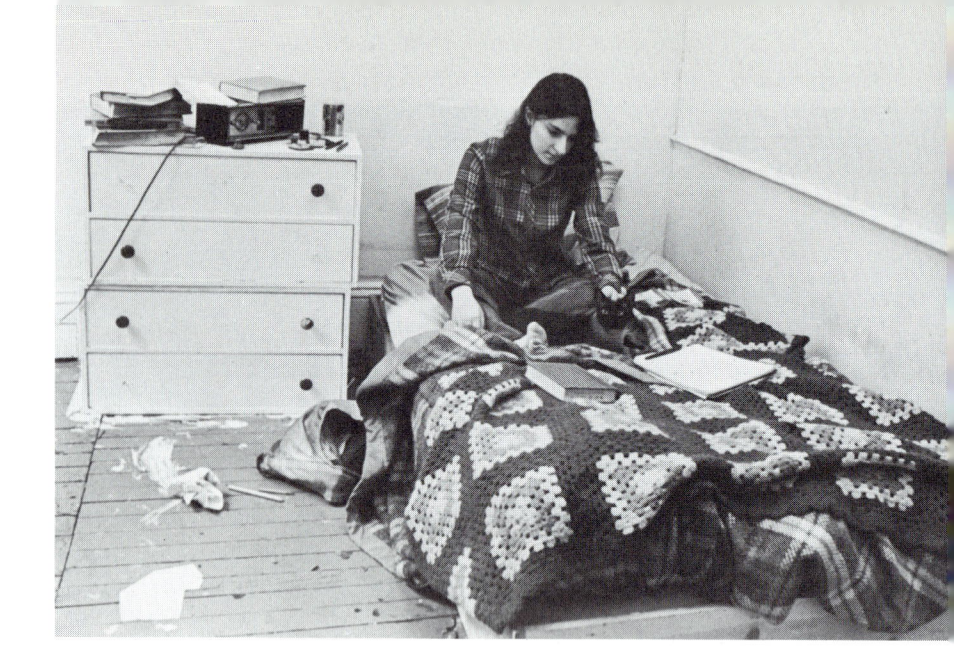

Using a Scale

To make a floorplan of the room you are working on, you will need a piece of graph paper with metric or standard divisions. Use metric if you measure the room in metric units, or use standard if you measure in standard units. You will also need a pencil, a ruler, and a carpenter's steel tape measure. If you don't have a carpenter's tape, you can use a meter stick or a yardstick.

Drawing to Scale

The first step in making a floorplan is to decide on a scale for your drawing. In order for your map to be an accurate reflection of your room, each square on your graph paper must stand for exactly the same measurement of real space. The relationship between the real space and the graph-paper square is called *the scale of your floorplan*. There are many different scales you can use but it would be best to use one that changes easily from the real measurement to the drawn measurement. The scale must also fit the paper you use. An easy scale to work with is 10 centimeters equals 1 meter (10cm = 1m). Another easy scale is 1 inch equals 1 foot (1″ = 1′). Both of these scales will require paper that is larger than 216 millimeters by 279 millimeters (8½ by 11 inches). Buy graph paper that is 279 millimeters by 432 millimeters (11 by 17 inches) or tape two pieces of 216- by 279-millimeter (8½- by 11- inch) paper together along the long edge. Make sure the lines on the first sheet line up exactly with the lines on the second sheet. If you want to use only a single sheet of the smaller sized paper the most convenient scales to use would be 4 centimeters equal 1 meter (4cm = 1m), or ½ inch equals 1 foot (½″ = 1′).

In the picture at left, the room is disorganized and unfocused. Colorful art objects, a comfortable area rug, and a simple shelf help bring the room together. What other changes might make an improvement?

Begin by using the carpenter's tape to measure the longest wall in the room. Suppose you find it is 3.81 meters (12½ feet) long. Write down this distance on a piece of paper. Next measure the width of the room. Suppose you find it is 2.74 meters (9 feet) long. Write down this distance also. Measure carefully and work slowly. Knowing the length and width, you can lay out the outline of your room to scale on the graph paper. The length will be represented by 38.1 centimeters and the width by 27.4 centimeters. To convert the actual

The furniture in this one-room space is now attractively rearranged to serve personal and social needs.

distance (meters) to the scale distance (centimeters) move the decimal point one place to the right. In standard dimensions the length is represented by 12½ inches and the width by 9 inches. If your room has a *jog* (a place where it angles in or out) measure the jog and include it in your floorplan.

Next measure the door locations in the room. Suppose a door is 0.9 meters (3 feet) wide and 152 millimeters (6 inches) from a corner. Since your metric scale has a ratio of 10 to 1, divide the actual millimeter distance (152) by 10 to get the scale distance (15.2). Find the spot that is 15 millimeters (you will not be able to measure 15.2 millimeters exactly), or ½ inch if using standard units, in from the corner of your plan. Put a mark there to indicate the beginning of the door opening. Then put another mark 9 centimeters or 3 inches from the first one. This indicates the end of the door opening. (See the illustration on page 65 for an idea of how professional designers indicate doors on their floorplans. You can adopt their system or use one of your own. The important thing is to be sure that you do mark them.) It is also important to show on your floorplan whether doors swing into the room or out of it. Again, use the symbols shown in the illustration or use your own system.

When the doors are all indicated on your floorplan, follow the same procedure and mark in the windows.

Finally, you should indicate the locations of electrical outlets on your plan. Find them in the room, measure their locations, and use a symbol to mark the locations on your plan (you can use an X if you like).

Your finished floorplan will be an exact drawing of the shape of your room, reflecting all the room's significant architectural features.

Using the same scale as you used for your floorplan, cut furniture shapes from another piece of graph paper. For example, if your bed is a standard 1.8 meters (6 feet) long and 1 meter (3½ feet wide,) cut a graph-paper rectangle 18 centimeters long and 10 centimeters wide (6 inches by 3½ inches) and label it "Bed". Now you can move the paper bed around the floorplan to see where it will fit in the room. Make similar cutouts for every piece of furniture you know you will be using in the room and for all furniture you might add.

ARRANGING FURNITURE FOR USE

There was a time when houses had many more rooms than the typical house has today. Each room was designed to serve a particular function. Kitchens were for cooking in and dining rooms were for eating in. There were sitting rooms, libraries, game rooms—even rooms that were meant only for music or only for sewing. Today, things are very different. Most rooms in our houses and apartments are expected to serve many functions. A kitchen may not only be for cooking, but also for eating, watching television, playing games such as Monopoly and bridge, and even visiting. At the same time, a kitchen may be a place to do laundry (washing, drying, ironing), may be a place to store food, or may be a place to do "desk work" such as using the kitchen table to write checks for bills and for writing menus. Obviously, arranging furniture in a room that has many different functions is a bit more complicated than arranging furniture in a room that has only one or two purposes. A multifunctional room requires more thought and careful planning.

Decide on Function

You began your consideration of your furniture needs by deciding what functions that furniture was to serve. Similarly, the first step in planning furniture arrangement for that room is to make a list of the functions that room is to serve. List the functions in the order of their importance.

In listing the uses of a given room, not everybody will come up with the same number of uses. For example, everyone will agree that a bedroom will be used as a place to sleep and dress. But beyond that, each person will have different ideas from every other person. Some people study in their bedrooms, while others prefer to do their studying in other rooms. Some people entertain groups of friends in their bedrooms, listening to records and just talking, while others do not. Some people think of their bedrooms as workrooms or hobby workshops. It is important to know for what you intend to use a room. Only with such knowledge can you arrange the furniture to help you obtain maximum use from the room you are designing.

It is also important to list the uses of a room in the order of their importance. For example, people in some households enjoy playing board and card games or working on jigsaw puzzles as a regular recreation. Others play cards or games only once in a great while. In arranging living-room furniture for the first household, you would want to include a table in a well-lighted area as one of the major furniture placements. For the second household, you might not include a table at all. Instead, you might choose a fold-away table that could be stored until it was needed.

Beginning with the most important function on your list, decide which major piece or pieces of furniture are necessary. Then list the minor pieces of furniture that are needed to complement the function of the major piece or pieces. A sofa needs a table nearby—either an end table or a low coffee table. A piano needs a piano bench or stool and perhaps a cabinet for sheet music.

Next, make a similar list—major piece, minor pieces—for the second most important function your room is to serve. Plan for all of a room's functions in this way.

Today, many rooms are multifunctional. What different functions are suggested by the objects in this room?

Group into Clusters

When your list of needed furniture is complete, study it carefully. You will find that the same kind of furniture is frequently needed for more than one activity on the list. If you arrange pieces in careful relation to each other, one piece of furniture can be useful in more than one way.

For example, suppose you have listed a desk and chair as being needed for studying, and a table and two chairs as being needed for playing your favorite game, Scrabble. If the desk were a flat-topped desk placed with its short end against the wall and with a chair on either side of it, that grouping could serve for *both* studying and Scrabble. Similarly, there is a way to arrange the major seating furniture in a room so that it is suitable for both conversation and television watching.

After you have reorganized your function list into three or four clusters of related furniture groupings, you must begin to think about where in the room each of those furniture clusters should go. To a large extent, this will be determined by your floorplan.

Where are the electrical outlets? Reading lamps, stereos, television sets, and the like must be positioned near enough to the room's electrical outlets to be easily plugged in. (Extension cords give you some flexibility, but it is generally wisest to position electric appliances as near to the outlets as possible.)

Where are the windows? Any activity that would benefit from natural light—desk work, for example—will dictate placement of furniture.

And once the locations of a few pieces of furniture have been determined by these fixed limits of your floorplan, the remaining pieces begin to "fall into place" by themselves. Obviously, chairs and sofas need to be placed where those sitting in them can see the television set without obstruction. Easy chairs for reading need to be positioned next to lamps, and then the location of the tables that those easy chairs demand will be determined.

A comfortably sized conversation grouping in the center of the room leaves the wall free for art collections and plants.

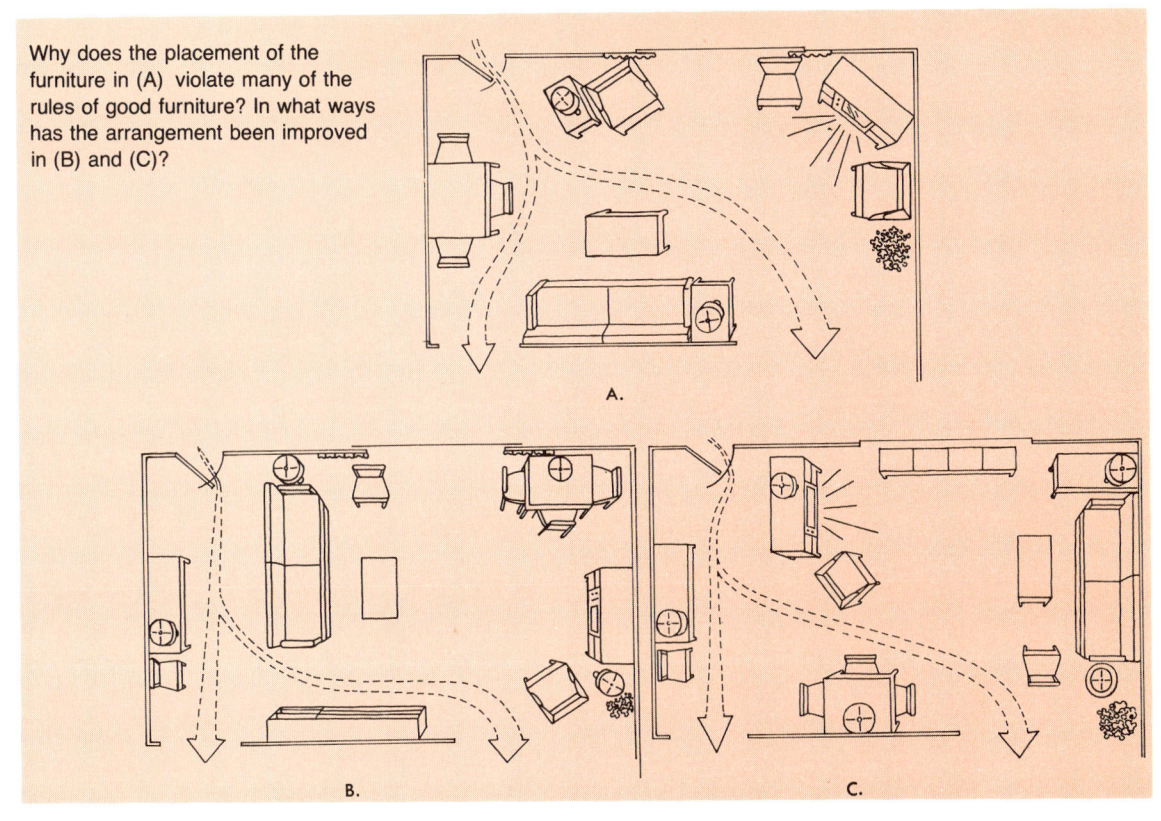

Why does the placement of the furniture in (A) violate many of the rules of good furniture? In what ways has the arrangement been improved in (B) and (C)?

A.

B.

C.

Any grouping of furniture for conversation must take into account the fact that communication is a matter of facial expression as well as words. People must be able to look at each other. For that reason, chairs and sofas must never be arranged in a straight line. Instead arrange them in an L, a semicircle, a circle, or a square. That way, people can face each other comfortably, and the group will have a cozy, intimate feeling.

Keep moving the paper cutouts of furniture around on your floorplan. Try one combination and then another until you are satisfied that the arrangement you have worked out is the one that best meets the needs of the room you are designing. But do not paste those furniture shapes down yet. Planning furniture arrangement according to function is the first step, but it is not the last.

ARCHITECTURE AND FURNITURE ARRANGEMENT

Doors, windows, and built-in furniture such as bookshelves and china cabinets affect your decisions about furniture placement. If you have drawn your floorplan carefully, it will show these architectural features clearly.

Energy Tips

Place furniture far enough away from radiators, registers, return air vents, and air conditioners to allow for air circulation.

309

Before making your final decision about furniture placement, ask yourself questions such as these:

Will someone coming through a door walk right into a piece of furniture, or is there enough room between the door opening and the furniture nearest the door?

If the door swings into the room, have I allowed enough room for it to swing free, or will it bump a piece of furniture?

Is the furniture near the windows arranged in such a way that the windows can be opened and shut and the shades raised and lowered without unnecessary bending and stretching?

Is the furniture arranged in relation to the windows, so that light coming through the windows is used to advantage?

Have I positioned furniture that will be used with stored items near the built-in storage units? (For example, dining tables require dishes and silver; desks require books; and game tables require game equipment.)

A special architectural feature of a room is a fireplace. If the room you are designing has a fireplace, you will need to give some extra thought as to how the furniture can best be arranged to take advantage of it. Because a fireplace and mantle are such a *conspicuous* (prominent) feature of a room, you will usually want to arrange the furniture in such a way that the main seating group faces the fireplace. That makes the fireplace the *visual focal point,* or center, of the room.

Controlling Traffic Flow

A final architectural consideration affecting furniture placement is *traffic flow.* Traffic flow refers to the pattern of movement people generally follow in going from one part of a room to another and from one room to another. As a rule, people will move in a straight line if they are free to do so. Generally, that makes the most sense. So, you do not want to arrange furniture in a room in such a way that it becomes an obstacle course to people moving from one part of the room to another. Check your floorplan to see if people can circulate easily within the room itself. Also be sure they can go from the room to the rest of the house without obstacles.

On the other hand, sometimes you deliberately want to encourage people *not* to move from one spot to another in a straight line. Suppose, for example, that your living room opens directly to the outside without an entry hall to separate the room from the apartment corridor or the out-of-doors. Anyone entering the room through the main door would be likely to cut diagonally across the room to a grouping of comfortable seating furniture without going first to the

---

Energy Tips

Never use charcoal in the fireplace. It gives off large quantities of carbon monoxide when it burns and has been a source of death when used for emergency heating. Its smoke does not always go up the chimney. Even a small hibachi gives off harmful levels of carbon monoxide.

The arrangement of furniture in functional groups can give a sense of architectural division in a large room, yet still retain the feeling of natural spaciousness.

coat closet. To encourage people coming into the room to move to the coat closet first, you can channel their movement by the way you arrange the furniture.

In addition to controlling traffic patterns, you can also use furniture arrangements to help overcome architectural problems. Rooms that are too narrow can be made to seem wider by placing large, important pieces of furniture (bookcases, chests, cabinets) at either end to reduce the apparent length. Another way to reduce the apparent length is to position a piece of furniture with its short end against the long wall. Because it juts out from the wall, a furniture piece positioned in this way will "stop the eye" of anyone entering the room. This will make the room look wider than it is.

Energy Tips

A thermostat that is near the heat from a fireplace may register a temperature that does not activate the heating source for the rest of the house. Fuel is automatically saved without your lowering the dial.

With some fireplace chimneys, it is possible to use more fuel—not less—when both the furnace and fireplace are going. When a fireplace is in use, possibly more hot air escapes from the room up the chimney than radiates from the fireplace into the room. More heat must then be generated from the home heating source to the rooms to make up for the heat lost from the fireplace.

Keep the damper closed when there is no fire in the fireplace.

One view of this studio apartment shows the dining area which also serves as a work area and library. Persian prints add both artistic flair and color to the monochromatic color scheme.

ARRANGING FURNITURE FOR BEAUTY

There is a tendency among some beginners to line up all the furniture around the walls of a room. An all-around-the-edges room looks awkward, stiff, and uninviting and should be avoided.

A few pieces of furniture such as a bed or chest of drawers *must* be located against a wall. Frequently, there is just one wall in the room where they will fit. Once those pieces have been placed, however, you have a certain amount of flexibility.

Formal Balance

One way to check whether your furniture arrangement is likely to be attractive is to consider the matter of balance. There are two types of balance. *Absolute,* or *formal, balance* is the kind you see when you look at two children of the same size sitting on either end of a seesaw. In a room, this kind of balance is achieved by drawing an imaginary line down the middle of the room or the middle of a furniture grouping. Then, place on either side of that line the same elements in the same relative position. Suppose, for example, that centered on the short wall of a living room is a large picture window. If you centered a sofa under that window, placed twin end tables at either end, and topped those tables with matching lamps, you would have formal balance. Formal balance in furniture arrangements is very restful to the eye. It also tends to look rather elegant (and sometimes a bit stiff). On the other hand, a little formal balance goes a long way. A room completely balanced on this "matching twins" basis would be very boring to look at.

ACCESSORIES AND DESIGN

The number of accessories in a room helps establish the feeling there. The spare furnishings and limited color in the modern living room above creates a cool, formal feeling. On the left, the greater number of accessories in this bedroom, with its print fabric, plants, and carefully placed wall art, conveys a more relaxed and comfortable environment. The great number of plants, objects, and art works in the room on the right suggests a feeling of warmth and individuality.

313

Plants and Design

Decorating with foliage and flower arrangements brings the natural beauty of plants inside your own home. In the picture above left, plants are used to soften a harsh and unappealing view outside the window. In the picture above right, plants are the primary dramatic focus of the entire room. In the living room below, plants are part of an overall restrained and formal design.

The living area above suggests that the owner is deeply involved with plants. The room is designed for living with and displaying the many varieties of plants. The red velvet of the couch provides a dramatic complementary color to the green foliage. The plants shown in the kitchen-dining area below serve to soften the rugged architectural materials of stone, wood, and brick.

Coordinating Furnishings

This multifunctional studio apartment provides seating, dining, shelf space, and table surface in a very small area. A unity of design is established by coordinating the wall covering and the fabric of the furnishings.

The bold and colorful design of these blue-and-yellow-print bedspreads is repeated on the walls and the ceiling. This dramatic ceiling treatment has the effect of lowering the ceiling and also creating a unity of design.

Decorative unity is achieved by the skillful use of the same floral-print fabric for the draperies and the bed linens.

Lighting

A side skylight lets in an ample amount of natural light to this sun-and-plant-filled living area. In the room below, a warm and intimate environment is created by the hidden light sources located in the shelving unit, in the recessed ceiling light, and in the small spotlight.

Recessed spotlighting on the ceiling of the remodeled stable above effectively and attractively lights a large space that gets a limited amount of natural light. The light fixtures in the room on the right are mounted on tracks. Track lighting is often used when an overall illumination is required.

The design elements of good natural lighting and a skillful floor plan are combined in this multifunctional kitchen, dining, and living area to produce a pleasing environment.

Informal Balance

The second kind of balance is called *occult,* or *informal, balance.* If you see two small children at one end of a seesaw and a much larger child balancing at the other end, you will be looking at an example of informal balance. It is the balancing of unlike things. In the example of the living room cited above, if you replaced one of the end tables and lamps with a small chest of drawers topped by a row of tall books and a low bowl of flowers, you would have informal balance. The chest, books, and flowers would balance the end table and the lamp. But you would have a balance of unlike things. Informal balance helps give a furniture arrangement interest.

In the chapter on knowing furniture, you learned how to look for harmonies in furniture size. But in grouping furniture, the greater variety you can bring into a grouping, the more attractive the room will be. You can often achieve both harmony and variety by creating an optical balance. For example, when a grouping of low seating furniture, such as a sofa and chairs, faces a large, elegant breakfront, an optical balance can be created by hanging an arrangement of pictures above the sofa. The pictures will then visually balance the height of the opposite breakfront.

A final principle to help you arrange furniture for beauty is this: Large pieces should be placed either against walls or at right angles to walls, while small pieces may be placed at an angle. Thus, the large pieces will parallel the walls of the room and lend architectural harmony of line. The more casual placement of smaller furniture (chairs and their accompanying tables) will keep the room from looking stiff.

Careers
Hotels, housing projects, colleges, hospitals, and institutions offer careers in furnishings or housekeeping management. The administrator's duties are to see that rooms are clean, attractive,

safe, and properly furnished at all times. There are assistants to carry out many of the duties. An executive in the housekeeping or furnishings department receives high pay and is often on a high level of management.

The administrator must be able to get along with all types of people; have problem-solving abilities; work within an annual budget; and be efficient, resourceful, and organized. A person who chooses this career must almost always have a college degree. Courses which prepare for administration in furnishings and housekeeping are home economics, accounting, human relations, business administration, textiles, and interior design.

Entry-level jobs are available in hotels and office buildings.

Learning Experiences

1. Using the floorplan shown on page 309 and as many furniture cutouts as you need, prepare *three* different furniture arrangements, all of which would be successful.
2. Prepare a floorplan of your room at home. Be sure to draw it to accurate scale. Include the furniture items in your plan.
3. Using a photograph of a room design that you find attractive, prepare a rough sketch of a floorplan, indicating the placement of all items in the photograph. Supply your own ideas about walls and furniture not shown in the photograph, and show their placement in your floorplan sketch. Measurements need not be precise, but they should be roughly to scale.
4. Find a photograph of a room in which the furniture is arranged according to principles of formal balance and another in which the furniture is informally balanced. Discuss the ways in which balance is achieved in the two room designs.
5. Prepare an alternative furniture arrangement to the one of your room as it is now (Exercise 2, above). Explain why you think the new arrangement is or is not an improvement on the existing arrangement.

CHAPTER 7

Fabrics and Window Treatments

One of the most bewildering problems facing the first-time interior designer is deciding on the best decorative treatment for the windows of a room. So many different elements need to be considered! These elements can be grouped into four considerations: fabric, function, architecture, and eye-appeal.

In this chapter, each of the different elements will be discussed. Most—though certainly not all—window treatments involve some use of fabric; so we will begin there.

FABRICS

To help you realize the importance of fabrics, imagine a room with no fabrics in it! Think how bare the windows would look, how hard the furniture would look, and how stark the whole room would appear. It is only when fabrics are put into a room that it begins to look inviting, warm, and homelike.

Natural Fibers

Fabric may be made from natural fibers or from synthetic fibers. Of the natural fibers, silk is generally considered to be the most beautiful. It is also the most expensive. Silk fibers come from the cocoons of silkworms raised specifically for the fabric industry. Cultivated silk fibers can be turned into fabric that is rich and heavy or light and sheer.

Wool is the most common animal fiber. It has certain qualities that are very desirable in a home-furnishings fabric. Wool takes and holds dye beautifully. It is water-resistant and can be easily cleaned. It also retains warmth better than most

The curtains on these windows can create an effect of one large window when there are actually three.

other fibers of similar weight. Nowadays, it can be chemically treated to make it mothproof and stain-resistant.

The most common vegetable fiber, cotton, is made into fabrics for countless household purposes. Cotton is comparatively strong, and it takes color well. It is also washable. Today's cottons are often chemically treated so that they are both wrinkle-resistant and quick-drying.

Linen is another popular fabric made from natural vegetable fibers. Linen lacks *elasticity* or "give." This makes it better suited to straight, tailored uses than to situations in which a flowing or gentle draping effect is desired. Linen has a natural crispness, strength, and luster—valuable qualities for fine

---

Energy Tips

Draperies, like storm windows, trap dead air, thus adding warmth to a room. The best fabric for blocking cold air is *closely woven* material. Fabric is closely woven if you cannot see light through it when it is held up to a sunny window. Draperies should be lined with another closely woven fabric. Foam or reflective types of lining are very effective in preventing heat loss.

New fabrics designed to save energy are available specifically for lining draperies. They are designed to keep the cold air out in winter and cooled air in during the summer. In addition, the draperies will also last longer. Colors fade less rapidly, if at all, and fibers are not so weakened by the sunlight.

Fully closed heavy draperies can reduce heat loss up to 25 percent, provided they do not cover a radiator or hot air vent.

TEXTILE FIBERS FOR FABRICS AND FLOOR COVERINGS

Fiber	Chief uses	Characteristics	Care
NATURAL FIBERS			
Cotton	Household fabrics Carpets Drapery and upholstery fabrics	Versatile Durable Withstands frequent, hard laundering Easily ironed at high temperature Inexpensive	Limited only by finish, dye, and construction Generally may be machined-washed and dried Avoid risk of mildew
Linen	Table linens Drapery and upholstery fabrics Other household fabrics	Beauty and luster endure through frequent, hard laundering Does not shed lint More expensive than cotton Wrinkles easily unless treated to resist wrinkling Resistant to dye-type stains	Limited only by finish, dye, construction of item Iron at high temperatures; avoid pressing in sharp creases Avoid risk of mildew
Silk	Drapery and upholstery fabrics	Natural luster Strong Dyes well Moderately resilient, naturally resistant to wrinkles, readily returns to shape More expensive than man-made (filament) silky yarns	Dry cleaning usually preferable Careful hand laundry possible with some items Protect from prolonged exposure to light Can be attacked by moths, carpet beetles
Wool	Blankets Carpets Drapery and upholstery fabrics	Springs back into shape; requires little pressing Great versatility in fabrics Has insulating capacity increasing with fabric thickness; hence fabrics can be warm Long-wearing	Dry cleaning usually preferable Will shrink and felt in presence of moisture, heat, and agitation, as in laundry Must be protected from moths and carpet beetles
MAN-MADE FIBERS			
Acetate	Drapery and upholstery fabrics Fiberfill	Drapes well Dries quickly Inexpensive Subject to fume-fading	Will glaze and melt at a low temperature in ironing or pressing
Azlon	This experimental protein fiber group has not yet been used for decorator fabrics. Scientists continue to search for better fibers in this group which might be used for such fabrics.		
Metallics Gold Silver	Drapery and upholstery fabrics	Decorative threads	May tarnish May melt at low temperatures
Rayon (conventional)	Drapery and upholstery fabrics Some blankets, carpets, table coverings	Absorbent Inexpensive Moderately durable Lacks resilience; wrinkles easily Flammability a danger in brushed or napped fabrics	Dry cleaning often required Can be laundered, but does not withstand treatment that can be given cotton or linen Tends to shrink and stretch
Rubber Lastex*	Stretch slipcovers	High degree of stretch and recovery Damaged by oils and light	Wash frequently with mild soap or detergent Avoid constant overstretch
Spandex Glaspan* Lycra*	Stretch slipcovers	High degree of stretch and recovery Resists abrasion Resistant to body oils	May be machine laundered with warm water. Dry lowest heat, shortest cycle

General Characteristics of the Man-made Fibers Listed Below:
- Moderate to high strength and resilience
- Resistance to moths and mildew
- Sensitivity to heat in ironing
- Dimensional stability; resistance to shrinking or stretching
- Tendency to accumulate static electricity in cold, dry weather
- Nonabsorbency; easy to wash, quick-drying
- Resistance to nonoily stains, but body oils penetrate the fiber and are hard to remove
- Pleat retention because of thermoplastic qualities

Nytril and Vinal fiber groups are still in experimental stages. Nytril has been tried in blends where an elastic fiber is desirable and Vinal has been tried where a wool-like texture is desirable, but no serious application of these fibers to decorator fabrics has yet been developed.

Distinctive Properties

Acrylic Acrilan* Creslan* Orlon* Zefran* Zefkrome*	Carpets Pile fabrics Blankets	Soft hand Resistant to wrinkling High bulking power Silky texture, if desired Resistant to effects of sunlight	Remove oily stains before washing Waterborne stains easily removed
Modacrylic Dynel* Verel*	Deep-pile and fleece fabrics Carpets (in combination with acrylic)	Soft and resilient Resistant to wrinkling Resistant to chemicals Nonflammable	May be ironed at extremely low temperatures only
Nylon	Carpets Upholstery fabrics	Exceptional strength Excellent elasticity Permanent shape retention Woven fabrics often hot and uncomfortable to wear	Oily stains should be removed before washing Washes easily Care must be taken to maintain whiteness Press at low temperature
Olefin DLP* Herculon* Vectra*	Seat covers for autos, outdoor furniture Carpets	No water absorption Low melting temperature	
Polyester Dacron* Fortrel* Kodel* Vycron*	Curtains Fiberfill	Sharp pleat and crease retention Some have resistance to pilling Exceptional wrinkle resistance	Oily stains should be removed before washing Easily washable Care should be taken to maintain whiteness Needs little ironing or pressing
Saran Rovana* Saran*	Seat covers for autos, outdoor furniture Screening; awnings Luggage	Resists soiling and staining Resists weathering Flame-resistant	Blot stains; rinse with clear water Sensitive to heat
Vinyon	Mixed with other fibers for heat bonding	Resistant to chemicals, sunlight Nonflammable	
Glass Fiberglas*	Drapery fabrics	Nonflammable Resistant to wrinkling, sunlight Permanent shape retention	Drip dry Avoid all rubbing

*Trademark name.
Source: American Home Economics Association.

draperies. On the other hand, it is naturally absorbent which makes it subject to water stains and mildew. It also wrinkles easily.

Another natural material that is not technically a fiber-based fabric is used so frequently in upholstery that it should be mentioned here: leather. Leathers dye beautifully, are durable, and are moisture-resistant. Such leathers as cowhide and steerhide are very expensive. However, like wool, they are so durable that their high initial cost may, in some situations, be justified.

Synthetic Fibers

For the last 100 years, an ever-increasing number of synthetic fibers has been created in chemists' laboratories. These have extended the range of fabrics

| BURLAP | CHINTZ | LINEN | HOMESPUN |
| TWEED | SAILCLOTH | NEEDLEPOINT | SUEDE CLOTH |

The effective use of fabric depends in part on the characteristics of the fabric itself. Coarse, simple fabrics are perfect for contemporary, Provincial, or simple traditional rooms.

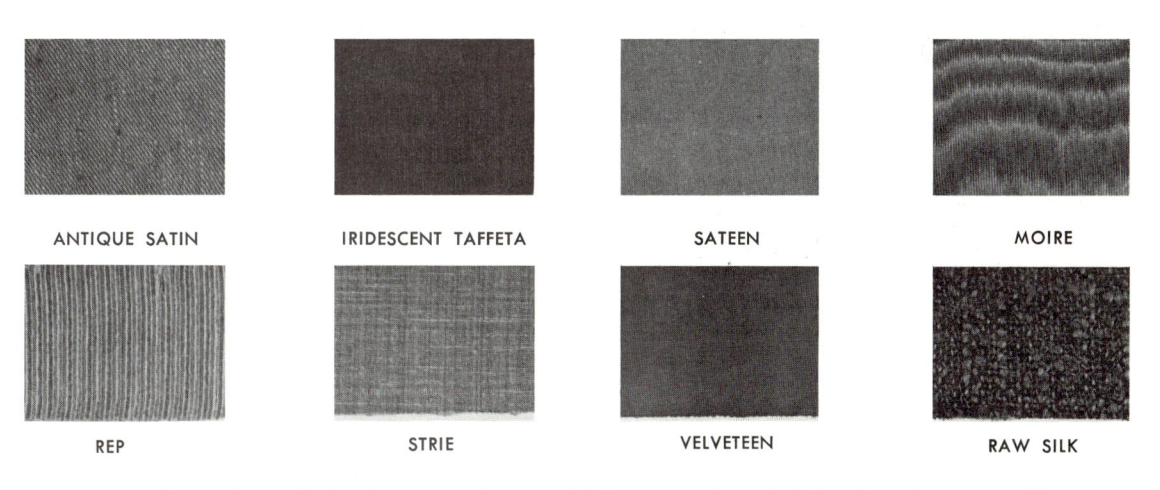

| ANTIQUE SATIN | IRIDESCENT TAFFETA | SATEEN | MOIRE |
| REP | STRIE | VELVETEEN | RAW SILK |

Depending on their color and quality, some fabrics can lend simplicity to a formal room or a little elegance to an informal room.

327

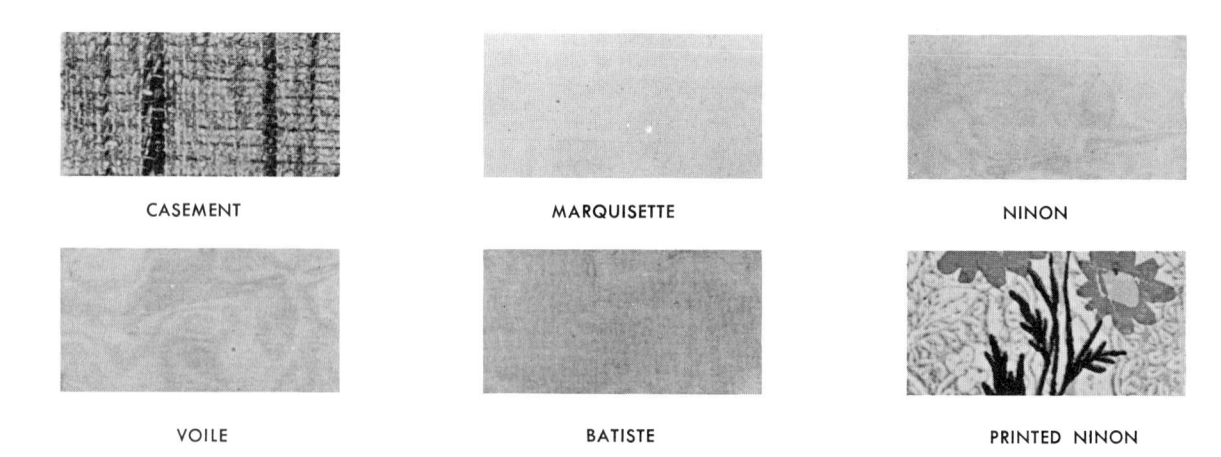

| CASEMENT | MARQUISETTE | NINON |
| VOILE | BATISTE | PRINTED NINON |

The effect of the semitranslucent fabrics and the sheer fabrics depends on their color and their tailoring. They can add an informal tone or a provincial simplicity to a room.

| BROCADE | DAMASK | MATELASSE |
| SATIN | TAFFETA | CUT VELVET |

The most elegant, elaborate fabrics are seldom appropriate in rooms that must serve an active family life.

available to the interior designer today. In fact, there are so many that it would be nearly impossible to list them all. What is more, new fibers are constantly being invented and introduced. It is worthwhile knowing that synthetic fibers have been classified into sixteen basic groups, each of which contains a number of fabrics. The chart on page 325–326 lists these groups and gives information about the special characteristics of each, as well as their special care requirements.

By law, all fabrics must carry labels giving basic information about their content and care. When you are considering a purchase of fabric, whether natural or synthetic, careful study of its label will pay big dividends.

Making Fabrics

The fiber from which the fabric is made is important. No less important is the method by which the fabric was made. The method of fabric construction affects the appearance, texture, and durability of the fabric. It also affects the cost.

Coloring Fabrics

How a fabric has been colored is another aspect of fabric construction that you need to know about. The easiest and least expensive coloring method is *piece dyeing,* in which the fabric is colored after it is woven. *Yarn dyeing,* on the other hand, involves coloring the yarns before the fabric is woven. Yarn dyeing offers more possibilities for color variation than piece dyeing. Yarn dyeing also makes it possible for a pattern to be woven with yarns of different colors. *Printing* is the third basic method of coloring fabric. In printing, color is stamped onto one side of a fabric. Because this treatment can add any number of colors to the fabric, it has infinite potential for variety.

Finishing Fabrics

In addition to coloring, the fabric surface is treated. Modern research has developed many new ways of *finishing fabrics;* that is, of treating the fabric surface. Fabrics may be finished so that they are durable-press and water-, soil-, or spot-repellant. They can also be permanently *glazed* (given a polished look) or treated to be wrinkle-resistant. Such finishes increase a fabric's usefulness and life span, and simplify its care. Study the labels on fabrics you are considering to see if they have been treated to improve their usefulness to your design scheme.

FUNCTION

A window serves two primary *functions,* or purposes. It admits and controls light and air. All window treatments should be planned to meet these needs.

If a window is designed to open, the decorative treatment of that window must not interfere with easy opening and closing of the window.

Energy Tips

For warmer climates, one type of glass commonly used is *thermopane,* a single pane which reflects heat. Another reflective insulation is *solar film.* The film is installed on the glass with a squeegee to make it smooth. The cooling savings will more than pay for the film in one season. It does, however, change the light.

An attractive window treatment of relatively little cost consists of cafe curtains and shades trimmed with bands of fabric. This tailored solution keeps privacy intact without cutting off light.

As for light, you must make a decision in terms of the particular window. Consider its location and the times of day in which the room is to be used. Most windows should be provided with some means of screening light, that is, controlling its flow into the room. Windows on the east side of a room will receive early-morning light. If the east room is a bedroom, you will probably want your window treatment to include a means of screening out that light in the early hours. On the other hand, windows on the west receive late-afternoon light—at some seasons of the year, a great deal of it. With that late-afternoon light comes a great deal of heat. If the room on the west is to be used in the late afternoon, you will want to consider a means of controlling that light and heat so that the room does not become unbearably warm.

There are two secondary functions of windows that also need to be considered. Both of them result from the fact that windows are transparent and thus "connect" the inside of a room with the outside.

The first of these secondary functions is privacy control. If a window is close to a neighboring building, a street, or a highway, determine the time of day when the room is used and decide whether it needs daytime or nighttime privacy. If you need to screen the room by day, you will want to choose a window treatment that lets in light while preventing outsiders from easily looking into the room. If nighttime privacy is desired, you will want to consider a window treatment that prevents any light from getting through. A curtain that admits light by day becomes more transparent at night when the inside is brightly lighted and the outside is dark.

The other secondary function you will want to consider is view control. If the view outside the window is an attractive one, you will want to design a window treatment that frames it but does not detract from it. On the other hand, if the view is unappealing, you will want to consider how your window treatment can minimize it or blot it out.

ARCHITECTURE

The way a window is constructed makes a great impact on your decision about its decorative treatment. *Fixed windows* (windows designed not to open) such as picture windows and the tall, narrow windows called *vision slots* generally present no mechanical problems. But when a part of a window is designed to open, the way in which it moves affects the possibilities for its decorative treatment.

Sash Windows Sliding sash windows are the most common type of window found today. The double-hung sash has two sections, each of which moves up and down. The ranch-style sash has two sections, each of which moves from side to side. Sliding sash windows can be treated with almost any type of fixed curtains or draw curtains and almost any type of top treatment. The one type of window treatment that interferes with sash windows is the type in which curtain rods are fastened to the inside of the window frame.

Swinging casement windows, which swing out like doors, are almost as flexible as sash windows as far as decorating goes. Fixed curtains, however, either attached to the window or hanging over the opening, would prove a clumsy choice for these casement windows. Such curtains would not be practical when the window is open.

Casement Windows. Casement windows that swing into the room, as opposed to those that swing outward, are more difficult to handle. Draw curtains can be used for such windows only if there is enough wall space on either side of the window to allow the curtains, when open, to hang completely clear of the windows themselves. And any top treatment for inward-swinging casements must be placed high enough to allow the window to be opened without its hitting the top treatment. Fixed curtains for inward-swinging casements must be fastened either to the window sash itself or hung from hinged, swinging-arm

The design of windows affects the way they should be treated. Bamboo shades can be used effectively on fixed windows. Plants nicely complement the brown tones of such shades.

Draw curtains work well on glass doors treated as windows.

brackets. This permits the curtains to be swung out of the way when the window is opened.

Awning and Jalousie Windows. Awning and jalousie windows have sections that are hinged at the top and open outward. They lend themselves to a variety of window treatments. The one unworkable treatment for such windows involves the use of fixed sash curtains. These are impractical here for the same reason that they are impractical on casement windows.

EYE-APPEAL

Types of Curtains

In most cases, you will probably choose to use some sort of curtains as part of your window-decorating scheme.

There are, in general, three types of curtains. These types, of course, can be made of endlessly different fabrics. They can be long or short. They can be looped, pleated, gathered, or straight. But despite the variety that these differences make possible, the three types remain constant.

Sheer curtains that hang next to the window glass are called *glass curtains*. Curtains gathered onto rods at top and bottom and attached directly to the window sash are called *sash curtains*. Other curtains are hung on a rod fastened across the middle of a window so that they cover only the bottom half of the window. These curtains may be called *cottage curtains, Dutch curtains,* or *café curtains*. Another style of curtains simply hangs loosely from a rod fastened above the window so that the curtains fall in gentle folds.

Glass curtains may be either a single panel of fabric or two panels hung side-by-side. When two panels are hung overlapping each other and are then tied back, they may be called *crisscross curtains* or *Priscilla glass curtains*.

The second type of curtain is the *draw curtain*. Panels of fabric wide enough to cover the window are attached to a rod in such a way that they can be drawn back and forth. They may be lined or unlined, *translucent* (admitting light) or *opaque* (admitting no light). When opened as wide as possible, draw curtains hang in folds that cover, or are hung just inside, the window casing. Draw curtains may be hung on a rod by rings which allows the curtains to be opened and closed by hand. Or they may be hung on an elaborate mechanical rod, called a *traverse rod*. To open curtains on a traverse rod, you pull firmly on a cord hanging near the window casement.

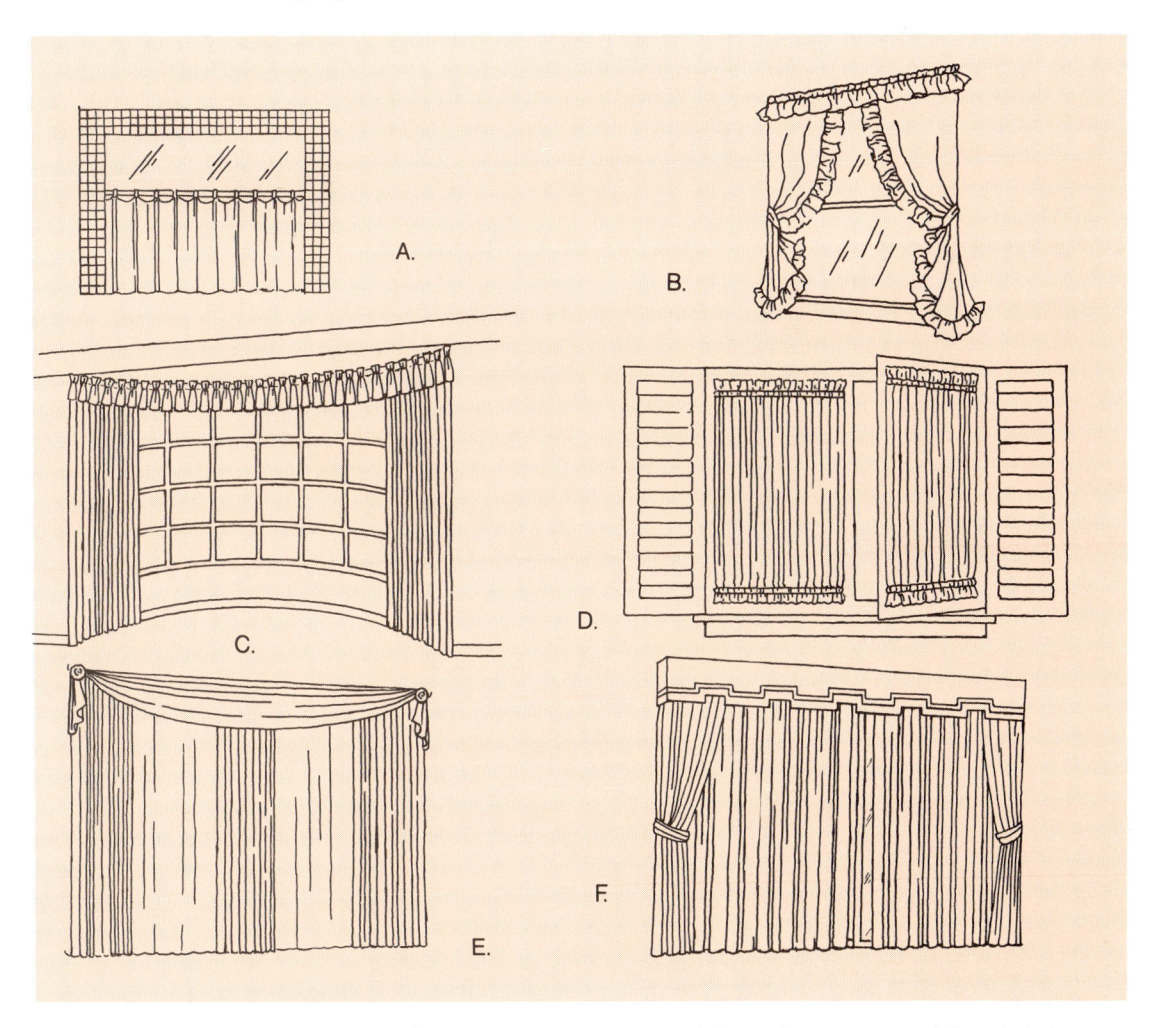

(A) A cafe curtain and frame give daytime privacy and decorative accent to an informal window.
(B) Shirred and ruffled glass curtains with a ruffled valance lend a cool, delicate feeling to a room.
(C) Translucent glass curtains and heavy draw draperies can be pleated and made to draw.
(D) Stretched sash curtains give practical privacy to windows. (E) Pleated glass curtains, combined with fixed draperies, lend daytime privacy and decorative accent. (F) Fixed draperies, looped back, and a lambriquin are combined with glass curtains for use on large windows.

Skilled use of the same fabric design for the wallpaper, bedspread, sash curtains, and overdrapery, bring a decorative unity to this bedroom.

The third type of curtain is the *overdrapery*. Overdraperies are panels of fabric that hang on either side of the window. They may be wide enough to draw closed, but sometimes, they are simply fixed in place at the sides of the window. Overdraperies are usually used with glass curtains or with semitranslucent draw curtains. The chief function of overdraperies is decorative.

Straight overdraperies are frequently used with café curtains or shutters in rooms decorated according to an informal, provincial theme. Looped-back overdraperies that do not draw are frequently used with glass curtains or draw curtains to lend additional elegance to a formal room. This type of overdrapery treatment is particularly effective for windows with a semicircular top, or to frame a dramatic view.

Choice of Window Fabrics

We have already considered in earlier chapters many of the questions you need to ask yourself when choosing a fabric for the window treatment you have in mind. The one warning to keep in mind when applying those earlier lessons about color, value, intensity, and pattern to a choice of window fabric is that it is important to visualize how your fabric choice will look when it is actually made into curtains. If the curtain style you have in mind involves fabric hanging in folds, you should consider whether the design of the fabric will look well when the panels of fabric are pushed together. If the curtains you are considering will be drawn over the entire window, you will want to consider how the fabric will look when covering so large a surface. Also, you will want to remember that the smaller an area, the more intense the color of a fabric can be. If you are curtaining just one window in a room, you can safely choose a bright, vividly patterned fabric. But if you are curtaining several windows in a room, it might be safer to choose a plain fabric or one with a less-intense design or color.

Types of Top Treatments

There are many ways in which you can treat the top of a window. If the room's ceiling is low, and the tone of the room informal, no special treatment may be needed. Curtains hanging from a simple rod may be the most effective arrangement you could choose for such a room. In other situations, however, you may prefer to supplement your choice of curtains with a special matching or contrasting treatment for the top of the window.

A *valance* is a gathered or pleated panel of fabric, usually matching the fabric of the draw curtains or overdraperies. It runs across the top of the window frame. A *lambrequin* is more formal than a valance. It is made of fabric that is stretched over a padded buckroom or plywood frame. Sometimes, the shape of the lambrequin is a severely straight rectangle. Sometimes, the top or bottom is beautifully shaped. It is hung from a rod or attached to a shelflike projection at the top of the window, and it covers the casing, the curtain rods, and the shades. The most formal fabric treatment of all for the top of a window is the *swag,* in which one or several lengths of fabric are looped into a decorative cascade with curving lines at the top of the window. Swags are appropriate only for the grandest, most elegant of room styles.

The valance, the lambrequin, and the swag all extend across the entire width of the window treatment and cover the tops of the side curtains. They can be hung at the top of the window casing or, if you want to add height, on the wall above it, so that the bottom of the treatment barely covers the window casing. In all cases, these top treatments completely hide curtain rods, window casing, and rolled window shades.

A fourth device that can be used to decorate the top of a window is a *cornice*. This is a long, boxlike form made of wood, metal, or mirror. It sufficiently projects into the room to cover the curtain rods and to allow the curtains to draw back and forth underneath it. It can be finished to contrast or match the drapery color or to match the woodwork. Sometimes, a cornice can also be used to cover and hide a fluorescent light that can dramatize the window and highlight houseplants in a window.

A fitted and shaped lambriquin and fixed overdraperies are combined here with translucent curtains.

SPECIAL TREATMENTS FOR PROBLEM WINDOWS

In general, if a window is pleasing in proportion and well placed on a wall, it should be accepted as it is. No effort should be made to change its height or width. However, if the window is not well proportioned or placed or if there are other special problems with the windows in a room, art and skill in selection of curtaining designs can make a tremendous improvement.

Widening a Window That Is Narrow. The appearance of a narrow window can be widened by setting opaque curtains against the walls on either side of the window. Position the curtains so that their inner edges just cover the window casing, while their outer edges extend several centimeters (inches) beyond the window frame. They will appear to widen the window because the viewer assumes that the window is as wide as the curtains.

Upholstered wallboard screens can be used in the same way. Hinge them to the window casing and keep them opened out over the wall. Shutters or sash curtains can be used with such window treatments to control light and privacy.

Increasing the Height of a Short Window. To add height to a window, place a top treatment on the wall above the window. Be sure that the bottom of the treatment covers the top of the window frame. Draperies extending to the floor will also help to fool the eye and add to the heightening effect.

Dealing with Different-Shaped Windows. When two windows in the same wall are different heights, a wide top treatment placed above the short window but hung normally over the long one will equalize their irregular heights.

If the windows are different widths, try putting draw curtains over the wall at the side of the narrower window, so that its uncovered surface matches in size the uncovered surface of its normally curtained, larger mate.

Dealing with Poorly Placed Windows. Some windows are so awkwardly placed that normal curtain treatments on them look a bit odd. Windows in stairwells or windows set high on the wall are good examples. If the window is small and privacy is not a necessity, consider leaving the window uncurtained. If it is a large window, curtain it to match the wall. If the window is sizeable and privacy is important, consider treating the window with shutters instead of curtains. Shutters painted to match the walls are far more inconspicuous than window curtains would be. They do not call attention to an awkward window.

Another kind of window that may require special treatment is the window set into or right next to a door. If complete privacy is desired at such a location, panels of opaque fabric can be a workable solution. Such panels can either be tacked in place over the glass or gathered onto rods fastened at the top and bottom of the windows. Where the need for privacy is not so great, glass curtains gathered on rods may be suitable.

Corner Windows. When windows form a corner of a room, there are several ways of handling them, depending on the style of the room. In a traditional-style

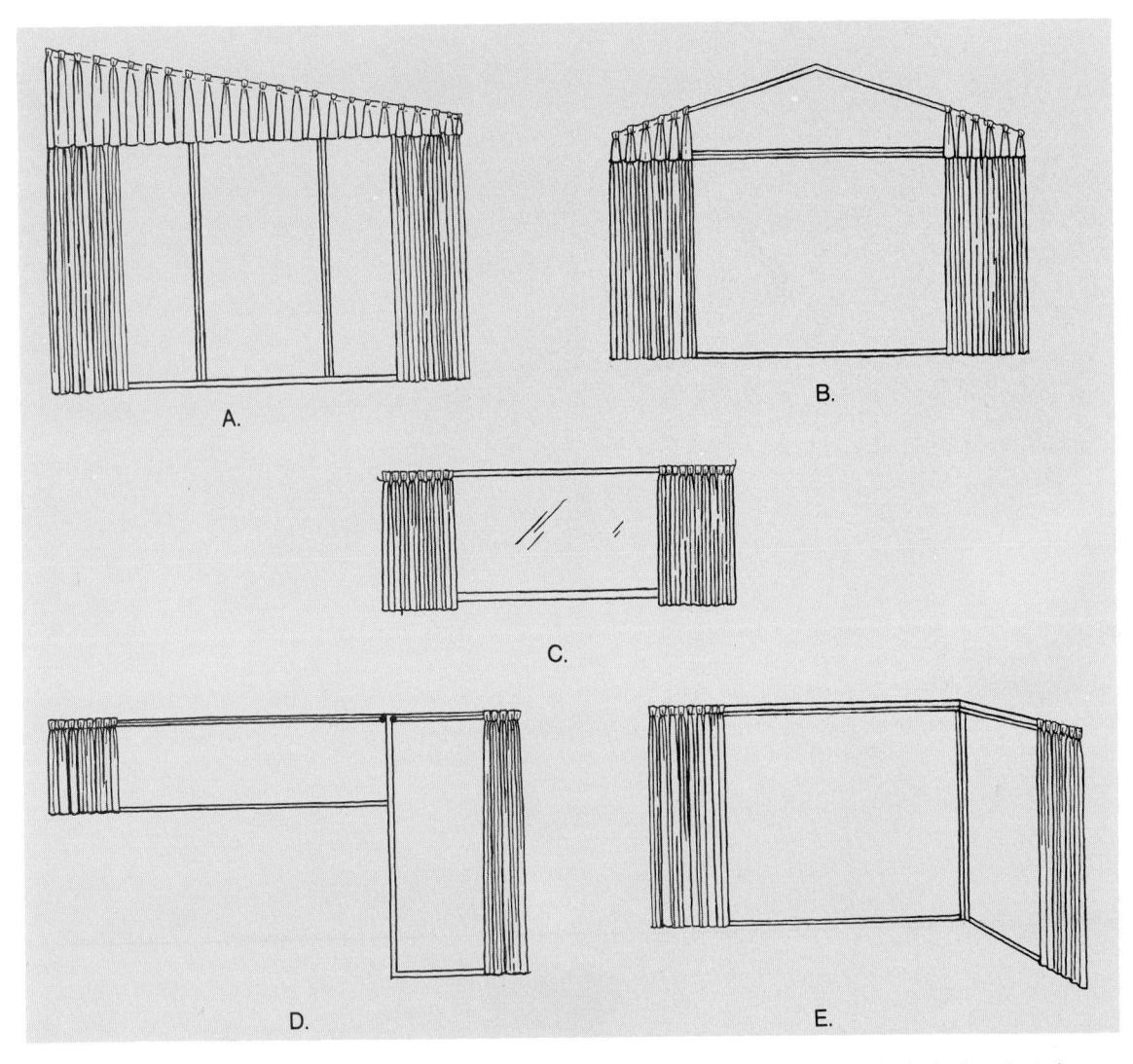

(A) Clerestory windows are left uncurtained; but where privacy or warmth is desired, a pleated valance can be used. (B) Clerestory windows with a peaked roofline can be left uncurtained, covered with a valance, or softened with a partial valance. (C) Ranch-type windows will look better if treated with simple traverse curtains. (D) Irregularly shaped windows, planned as architectural accents, should be accepted as they are, blending drapery and wall in color.
(E) Contemporary curtaining emphasizes the airiness of corner windows.

room, try handling the group as though it were made up of two separate windows, each curtained individually. In a contemporary-style room, curtain only the outer edge of the grouping.

OTHER TYPES OF WINDOW TREATMENTS

Curtaining, of course, is not the only way in which windows can be handled decoratively. Here are some other possibilities.

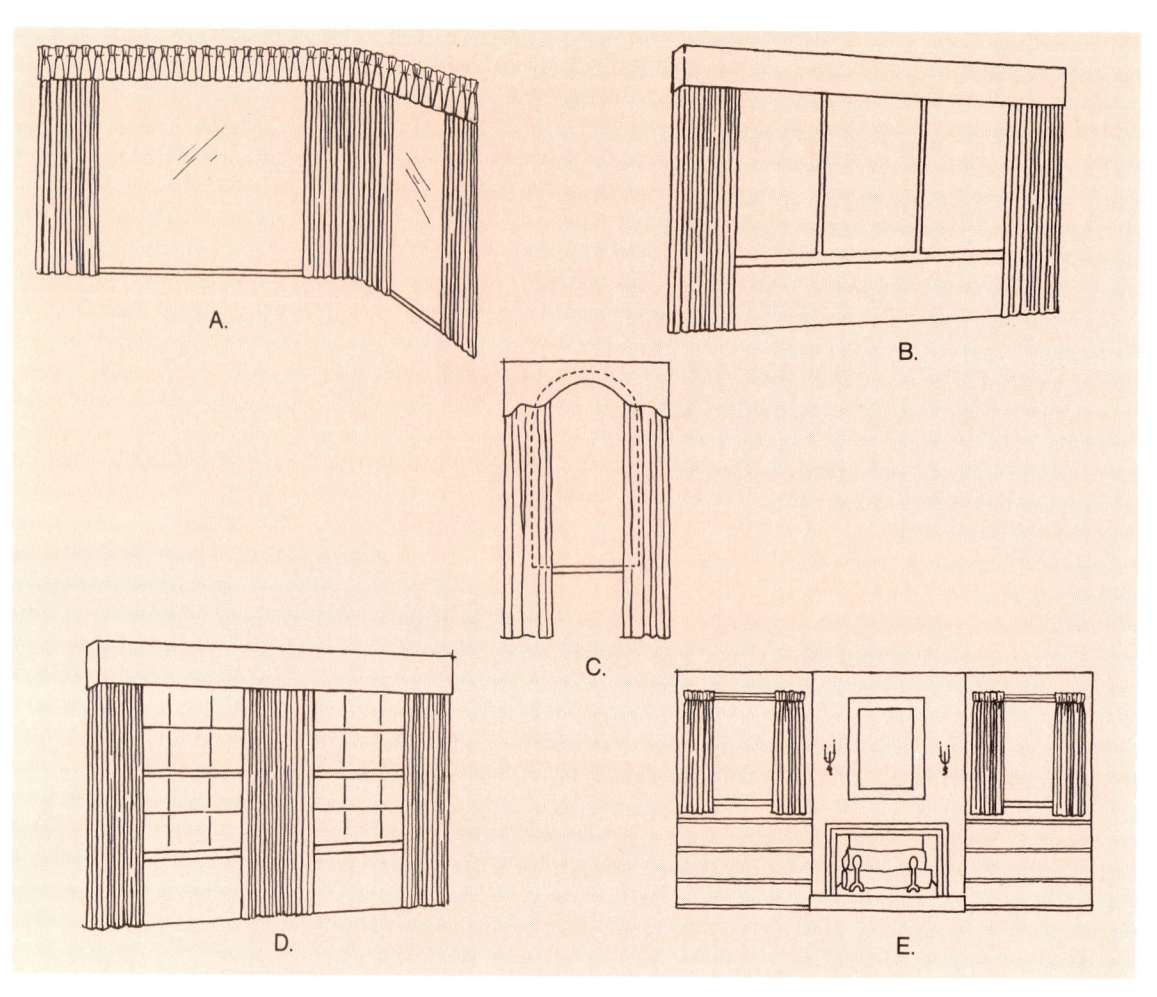

(A) Traditional curtaining of corner windows emphasizes the structural corner with draperies. (B) Groups of windows should be treated as one window wherever possible. (C) When draw curtains are desired on an arched window, the rod is place on the wall and the wall is masked with a shaped lambriquin or valance. (D) Windows separated by a wall space that is smaller than the width of a single window can be treated as a grouping by covering the wall with drapery and unifying the whole with a single top treatment. (E) Windows on each side of a fireplace can be inconspicuously draped with draw curtains that match the wall.

Window Shades. Coated-fabric window shades have always been an excellent way to handle the light and privacy of a window. Such shades roll up on an inconspicuous roller. When the window is a standard size, such shades are usually quite inexpensive. In the past, window shades were available only in a very limited choice of colors. Today, however, they have come into their own as a decorating feature. Shades can now be bought in a wide range of colors. There is also a do-it-yourself variety that enables you to fasten your own fabric to the shade. That way, your shades can harmonize with your curtains or can be used as the only decorative window treatment. Window shades are available in two basic weights. The semitranslucent weight admits some light. The semiopaque weight excludes most light. There are also special "room-darkening" shades on

The deep color of the window shade accented by a white geometric motif imaginatively repeats the color scheme of the crisp check fabric of the bedspread and three-paneled screen.

the market. These are designed to keep out almost all light, so that sleeping for night workers becomes no problem.

Shutters. Wooden shutters with moving slats are a practical way to control light, air, and privacy. Shutters can be finished in natural wood tones or painted. Shutters are also available with solid wood panels instead of moving slats. Another type of shutter is simply a frame designed to hold fabric of your choice. (You gather the fabric onto small rods set into the frame openings.)

Shutters require little maintenance and are practically indestructible. But they are also expensive. If your windows do not take a stock-size shutter, shutters can be very expensive indeed. Occasionally, you can adjust a stock-size shutter to the dimensions of your window with just a few simple woodworking tools—if you have the know-how. But other times, it is necessary to have shutters custom-made.

Venetian Blinds. Venetian blinds of wood, metal, or plastic are slatted shades that control light the way a shutter does. They are not only less expensive than

A bright geometric motif of the laminated shade cloth works wonders for a white kitchen.

These kitchen window shutters serve both as curtains and as a means of controlling light and privacy. They may be painted for a casual look that is appropriate in either traditional or contemporary rooms.

shutters, but easier to install. Today, venetian blinds are available in both horizontal and vertical styles and in a variety of colors. A problem with venetian blinds, however, is that they have a tendency to break easily in the system of cords and pulleys involved in raising, lowering, and tilting the slats. Also, venetian blinds tend to collect dust. Therefore, they are a maintenance problem for the housekeeper.

Split-Bamboo and Matchstick Curtains. Roll-up curtains or blinds of bamboo or bamboolike material are an attractive window covering for warm, informal rooms. Such blinds can be spray-painted to match any color scheme. They can also be used in their natural color to blend with light-colored furniture. They are

When shutters are finished in natural wood tones to match walls or to fit dramatic windows, they have great dignity and are appropriate in elegant interiors.

These vertical blinds add texture with a handwoven look and let in light without relinquishing privacy.

reasonably priced and easy to use. Many decorators find these curtains very attractive. They do not provide complete privacy, however; so you may want to supplement them with additional window coverings.

Screens. Wallboard screens, which are usually painted or covered with fabric or wallpaper, can be used dramatically as window coverings. They can be hinged to the casing or inserted into frames fastened to the walls around the window. They can also slide back and forth, controlling the light and providing complete privacy.

SHOPPING FOR WINDOW TREATMENTS

Much of what you have already learned about shopping for home furnishings and home-furnishings supplies will apply to shopping for window treatments. There are a few special hints that apply to this area of home decoration.

Matchstick bamboo curtains are inexpensive, good-looking, and allow light to come into the room.

Temporary or Permanent Curtains?

One of the important and determining factors in the selection of window treatments is how long they will be used. Will you be moving within a year or two? Or, is the home a permanent—or at least nearly permanent—one?

If you are buying curtains for a temporary home, you can approach the problem in one of two ways. You can spend as little as possible and plan to discard your curtains when you move. Or, you can invest in curtains that could be altered later for use in another home. The first alternative is a good one *if* you are able to find very inexpensive curtains whose colors, design, and style are acceptable to you. However, you will have to shop a great deal before you are likely to come up with such curtains. Even then, the quality is likely to be so poor that they still may not last for their desired life span. If you are skilled with a sewing machine, an alternative would be to find inexpensive fabric and make the curtains yourself.

If you choose to spend somewhat more money, plan to reuse your curtains in a later home. It would be wise to invest in quality curtains whose style, color, and design are fairly simple. That will increase the likelihood that they will be appropriate in a new situation when you move. In following this approach, remember that the curtains may not be used in the same type of room in your next home as the room for which you are now buying them. For example, suppose you are buying curtains to use right now on the two windows in your bedroom at home. In your first apartment, you may find that the bedroom has just one window; so the extra pair of curtains can be used in the bathroom or hall in your new apartment. For this reason, curtains that you hope to reuse in a new situation should be kept as simple as possible to ensure flexibility of use.

If you are in a home of a semipermanent nature, of course, you can afford to invest a greater amount of money in curtains or other window treatments. Their longer useful life will justify their higher cost.

Professionally Made Curtains or Homemade?

The decision to have professionally made curtains or homemade curtains is no longer a simple one. There was a time when homemade curtains were automatically less expensive than those bought ready-made. That is no longer always true. You will have to decide how important it is to you to have curtains in your own choice of fabric, style, and quality of workmanship. You will also have to consider the time and effort involved in making your own curtains.

Ready-made Curtains. Ready-made curtains are mass-produced in a limited range of lengths, widths, colors, patterns, and fabrics. They are sold in department stores and through catalog houses, usually at standard prices. That is, comparison shopping is not likely to turn up wide price differences. Ready-made curtains are generally the least expensive kind you can buy. Often they cost less than you would have to spend to buy the fabric alone. If your windows are close to standard size and if you are fairly flexible about the look of curtains, ready-made curtains could be your best choice. On the other hand, it is virtually

A more traditional room needs a more elaborate window treatment. The arched-framed windows in this formal living room are treated with overdraperies and translucent glass curtains.

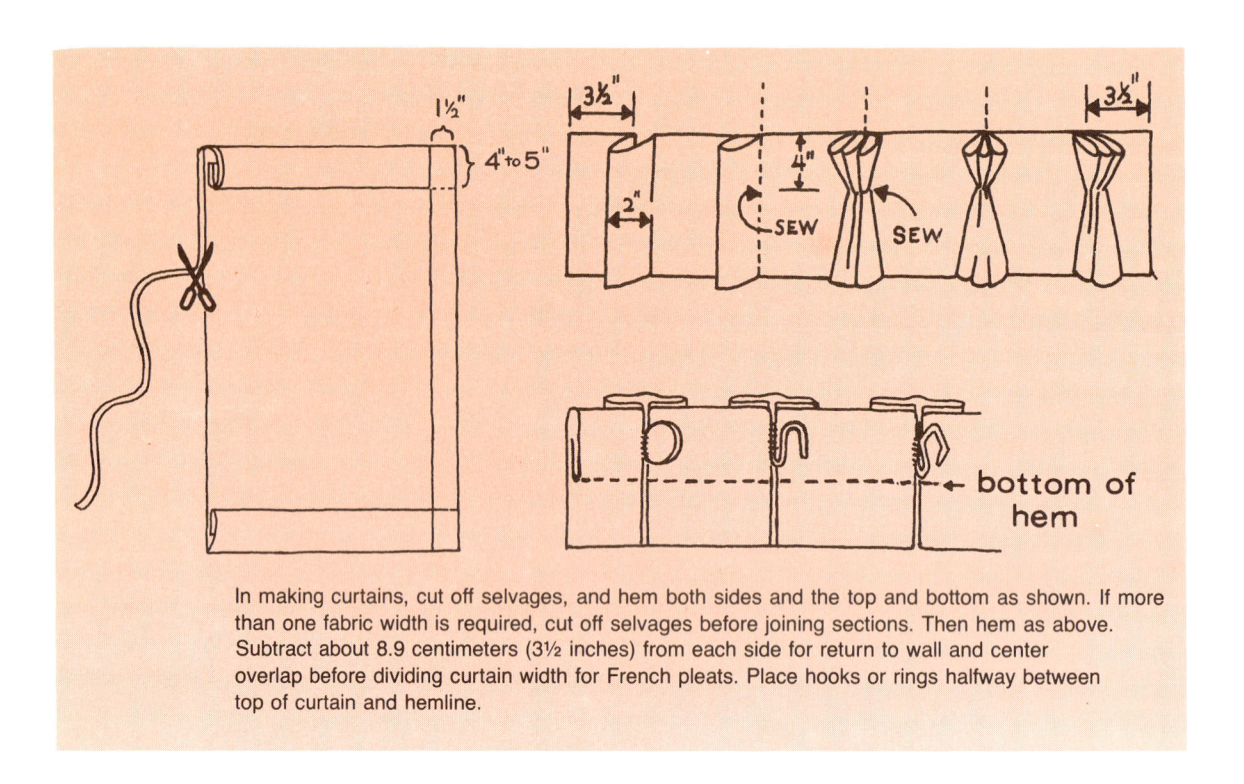

In making curtains, cut off selvages, and hem both sides and the top and bottom as shown. If more than one fabric width is required, cut off selvages before joining sections. Then hem as above. Subtract about 8.9 centimeters (3½ inches) from each side for return to wall and center overlap before dividing curtain width for French pleats. Place hooks or rings halfway between top of curtain and hemline.

impossible to find ready-made curtains for odd-shaped or odd-sized windows. Also, ready-made curtains, since they are meant to appeal to a wide variety of tastes, seldom have any special "zip" to their designs.

Semicustom-made Curtains. Semicustom-made curtains are also mass-produced. These, however, are usually available in a much wider range of lengths and widths. This means that you can order semicustom-made curtains that will come very close to being a perfect fit for your windows, whatever their size. The workmanship, the range of fabrics, and the selection of colors in semicustom-made curtains are all a cut above those in ready-made curtains. As you would expect, the cost of semicustom-made curtains is a bit higher than that of ready-made curtains.

Custom-made Curtains. Custom-made curtains are individually made to fit your windows. You select the fabric and decide the style. Since they are made only for you, such curtains are the most expensive kind of professionally made curtains you can buy. Generally speaking, the cost includes the measuring, the rods, hooks, and other necessary supplies, and the cost of the fabric. The price also includes the cost of labor in making the curtains and the final *installation* (hanging) of the curtains in your home. However, this is not *always* so. It is important that you know exactly what you will be getting for any price quoted to you for the making of custom curtains.

Homemade Curtains. Homemade curtains can be as costly or nearly as inexpensive as you choose. To a large extent, their quality will depend even more on your sewing skills than on the amount of money you spend. If you are good with a sewing machine and have the time to devote to curtain making, this could be a wise route for you to follow.

Before you make the commitment to the idea of homemade curtains, however, do some figuring. Write down the cost of fabric, but also, consider the need for special equipment. If you plan to make curtains for very large windows, you may need special tables for laying out so much fabric. You may also need special machines in order to sew it properly. Will you have to rent such items? If so, estimate their cost and write it down. If they are to be lined, have you included the cost of lining fabric? Will you need curtain rings? Will you have to buy lead weights to sew into the hems of draperies so that they will hang properly? The cost of pleating tape and pleating clips may also be a factor.

Preparation for Buying

The first step in preparation for a shopping expedition is to know the exact measurements of the windows for which you are buying furnishings. Look at the drawings below for help in figuring the exact *yardage* (length and width of fabric) you will need.

The other steps in preparing for a shopping trip have already been discussed in earlier chapters: carry color swatches with you, be prepared to ask questions and take notes, and so on.

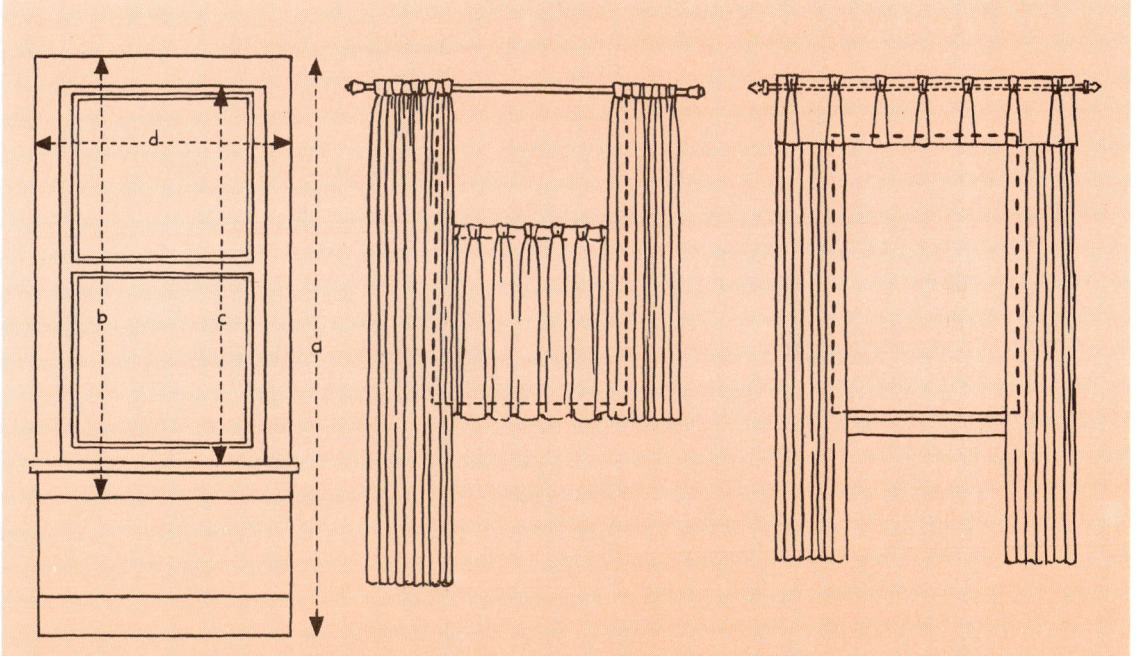

Draperies can hang from the top of the window casing (a) to the floor or (b) to the apron. Draperies must be wide enough to cover the casing (d). Glass curtains can be hung in the same way, or they can be recessed inside the casing and hung to the sill (c). Both long and short draperies can be hung beyond the window over the wall. Half-curtains provide privacy while allowing light to enter the room. Low windows can be raised, and different height windows can be made more uniform by placing a top treatment on the wall above the window.

345

Precautions about Hidden Costs

Most people check the tags on fabrics to learn about strength, firmness, soil resistance, and wrinkle resistance. You should always do the same. But there are other things for which you should look when considering a fabric for purchase.

What about cleaning? Will the curtains have to be dry-cleaned, or will they be washable? Remember, dry cleaning is expensive.

What about special hardware? The curtains displayed in the department-store showroom may look stunning. But that effect may depend on the handsome (and expensive) brass-finished rod on which they are displayed. You may not want to spend the amount of money the rod costs. If you are buying draw draperies, have you considered the cost of the traverse rod that will open and close them? If you are buying café curtains, do they come with loops or rings attached? Or, will you have to buy curtain rings and then sew them on by hand?

A misleading practice in shopping for curtains is that we tend to look at the curtain itself and to forget about all the other small-but-important elements that are included in the process of tailoring or actually installing curtains. Watch for those hidden costs as you shop for curtains or other window coverings.

Energy Tips

Sausage-shaped rolls (like bean bags) can be made to exclude drafts that find their way in at windowsills despite storm windows. Simply cut a strip of material a little longer than the width of the window and twice the width of the roll desired. Fold it lengthwise and sew the sides together leaving one short side open. Turn it inside out, stuff it with cotton or polyester, and sew the open end together by hand. The fabric can match the windowsill or blend with the draperies.

What factors must be taken into account in computing the cost of draperies like these?

Careers

Textile chemists develop and analyze new fabrics. They may create synthetic fibers or refine processes that improve known fibers. A textile chemist is interested in new fabric dyes and finishes, the durability or flammability of a fabric, and the way fabrics react to different cleaning methods. A college degree in chemistry is required, and a master's or doctorate degree is often preferred.

Textile designers create the design of a fabric. They specify the type of weave, the color of the dyes, and the *pattern,* or design. Textile design is a creative career. The designer must have some training in art and have a good sense of color. In addition, the designer must know about the technology of fibers, weaving, dyeing, and printing. Some designers specialize in a certain fabric or process. A college degree in art is usually required.

Learning Experiences

1. Prepare a bulletin-board display showing different types of windows and different types of window treatments. Choose one picture in the display that you think shows a treatment that could be successfully adopted or adapted for the windows in your room at home. Explain through words or sketches how you would actually apply the treatment.
2. Design a window treatment for a picture window looking out on an unattractive view.
3. Design a window treatment that provides for light, air, and privacy, as well as beauty.
4. Make a list of fabrics that can be used attractively in window treatments. Next to each, note the kind of laundering care the fabric requires and the possible styles for each.
5. Design a window treatment which does not include the use of fabric curtains.

CHAPTER 8

Accessories

A room can be completely furnished and yet be as stark, impersonal, and uninteresting as a motel bedroom or an airport lobby. Only when you put accessories into it does the room feel like your personal space. Accessories are small objects that are both useful and decorative. Lamps, pictures, plants, pillows, wastebaskets, and books are common accessories.

Many people do not give much thought to their selection of accessories for a room. They add a lamp here, an ashtray there, a vase in one corner, a clock in another. However, successful interior designers know that well-chosen accessories can "make" a room design, while poorly chosen accessories can "break" a room design.

Express Your Personality

Another reason that accessories should be chosen with care is that they, more than any other element in the room, express your personality. So, accessories should always truly reflect your own tastes, interests, and needs. If you hate abstract art, do not choose an abstract painting to decorate a wall even if you think that abstract art may be the fashionable style of the moment. If you enjoy an object—for instance, a tin can painted and covered with glued-on

---

Energy Tips

Spotlights placed outside a house are not necesary every night. They may be used for special occasions—to light an area used for entertaining—or for security. Using them every night to illuminate a part of the property that is not in use is a waste of energy. The least-expensive bulbs to use outdoors are mercury or low-wattage bulbs.

macaroni that your little brother made for you at camp—include it as an accessory in your room, whether it is fashionable or not.

Don't Go "Overboard"

Of course, the use of accessories can be carried to extremes. Too many accessories—no matter how tasteful, useful, and beautiful each is by itself—will lead to a look of disorganized clutter. So, do not overcrowd a room with accessories.

Another way accessories can fail is if they are chosen because they seem to underscore the decorative look of your room, rather than for their own beauty and usefulness. In some magazines dealing with home furnishings, you can find photographs of so-called *designer rooms*. Every accessory in the room has obviously been selected because it is the "right" style or the "right" color. Even the ashtrays and paintings match. Some inexperienced designers go even further, covering all the books in a bookcase with paper covers that match! Such rooms do not look like places where real people live. They look too perfect!

Accessories make it easy for you to express your own taste and ideas of what is beautiful. Taste is developed and refined through observation and experience. This development is a lifetime process. Part of that process involves learning to use your eyes. Pay attention to combinations of colors and shapes in the world around you. Notice textures. Ask yourself: Do I like the way this looks? Why or

---

Energy Tips

We use more lighting than we need. Turning off extra lights conserves energy. General Motors Corporation saved $900,000 a year on energy bills by turning off unneeded lights. A national chain of department stores turned off half the lights in all of their 350 retail outlets and saved 40 million kilowatt hours of electric energy. If one 150-watt bulb in an unused room in every home were turned off for two hours each evening, we could conserve 18 million kilowatt hours of electricity daily!

Pottery and wall hangings are popular accessories today. An appreciation for handmade crafts can be one expression of an individual's tastes, interests, and needs.

why not? Why do others find beauty here? What is the most attractive feature? Gradually, you will begin to *know* what things are beautiful and what things are ugly. Perhaps more important, you will begin to see how the relationship of one object to another can make those objects appear either attractive or unattractive.

LAMPS

Perhaps the most useful accessories in a room are lamps. The first question to ask when you consider a lamp is: Will it provide the kind of light that is needed? A lamp that does not give adequate light where light is needed is a poor choice, no matter how attractive it may be.

Different kinds of lamps are designed to meet different lighting needs. The two most familiar lamp styles in the home furnishings field are table lamps and floor lamps. In addition, there are:

spotlights—small, powerful lamps, used singly or in groups, mounted on a ceiling track

wall lamps—lamps either attached permanently to a wall or suspended from a wall by a hook or nail

ceiling light fixtures—ranging from fancy chandeliers to simple, enclosed fluorescent lights

recessed lamps—special lamps imbedded in a ceiling or hidden behind a window cornice

The placement of lamps will be determined to a large extent by the arrangement of your furniture. Each grouping of furniture will require its own source of light. The size and makeup of each grouping will determine the types and number of lamps that will serve it best.

Many rooms come with light fixtures in the ceiling known as *overhead fixtures*. Overhead lighting fixtures work well in kitchens and dining rooms, because they give the kind of general overall light those rooms require. But lamps are a better choice for living rooms and bedrooms and are used even when a ceiling fixture is already in the room. In living rooms and bedrooms, people tend to feel more comfortable in pools of light than they do in a room that is lighted to the same degree of brightness throughout.

Lighting can create atmosphere and give warmth to a room. The adjustable directional wall lamp on the left and the mounted ceiling light on the right are both examples of spotlighting.

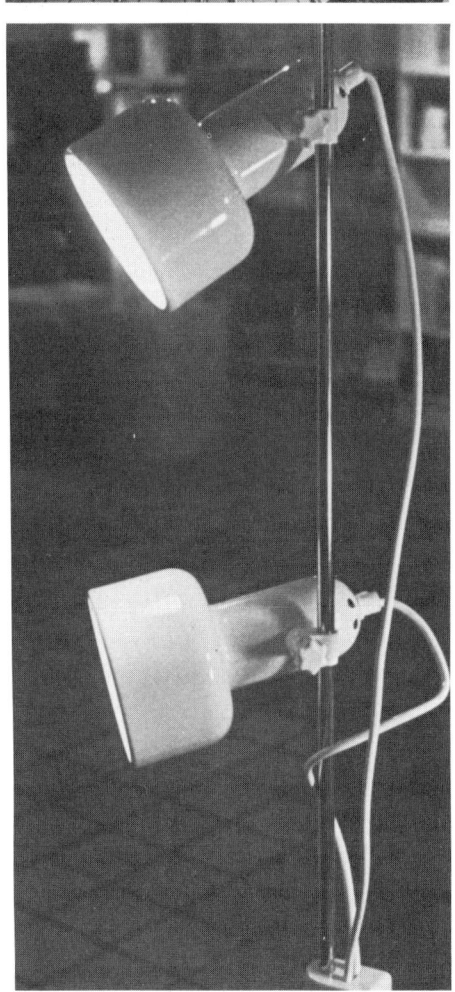

In addition to the wide variety of traditional lamps, there are many new design developments in contemporary lighting fixtures. (Top left) Theatrical-type spotlights used singly or in groups are mounted on tracks on ceilings or walls. (Top right) Oriental paper lampshades are another popular and inexpensive lighting solution for contemporary homes. (Bottom) Modern floor lamps made of plastics and highly polished metals reflect the existing technology.

Lamp types, placements, and light distributions. (Top) Ceiling lamps and floor lamps. (Second row) Spotlights and porch lights. (Third row) Wall mounted lamps behind reflectors and table lamps. (Fourth row) Hanging lamps and a fireplace as light sources. (Fifth row) Hanging lamps must be mounted to keep glare out of eyes. A reading lamp. (Bottom) Desk lamps should also be placed to avoid glare. A directional wall lamp.

Choosing A Lamp

In choosing a particular lamp, use the same tests that you would use in choosing a particular piece of furniture. First, look at the lamp in silhouette. Does the shape or outline of the lamp please you? Are the base and the shade in proportion to each other? If you are considering a table lamp, how will it look with the piece of furniture on which it is to stand? By itself, a tall, gracefully thin lamp may be beautiful. But it might look weak on a wide, low chest.

Next, consider the surface of the lamp. Will its color harmonize with the other colors in your scheme? Is the decoration on the lamp base appropriate, or is it too fussy? Does the surface of the lampshade harmonize with the surface of the lamp base? As a general rule, a lamp with a coarse or rough base looks best with a shade that is also roughly textured. Lamps with smooth, shiny bases look best with smooth, fine-textured shades.

In addition, there are some special considerations in choosing lamps that do not apply to choosing other pieces of furniture. The first is the question of whether your lamp should have an opaque or a translucent shade. This depends on personal preference and on how much light each lamp must provide. In a large, dark room, semitranslucent shades are often best. Semitranslucent shades allow a lamp to provide as much light as possible. In a small, light room with many lamps, opaque shades are frequently appropriate. Then, the lamp is needed for atmosphere and warmth. If you choose an opaque shade, be sure that the inside of the shade is white or off-white. This ensures that the reflected light is not colored. For the same reason, you should also choose semitranslucent shades that are white or off-white.

Lamps can be purchased in the lamp or furniture departments of many stores. But you can also find attractive, usable lamps at secondhand shops, antique shops, rummage sales, and other used-furniture outlets. Before buying used lamps, inspect their mechanical parts carefully. Check the sockets, switches, and cords. If there is any sign of damage, do not buy them; or plan to rewire them if you *do* buy them. Lamps with damaged wiring can cause fires!

Energy Tips

When light is needed for reading or other tasks, you may save energy by using one high-wattage bulb rather than several low-wattage bulbs. One 100-watt bulb produces about the same amount of light as two 60-watt bulbs. Never use a higher wattage bulb than the fixture specifies, or you may damage and shorten the life of the lamp.

In hallways and foyers, less light is required, but constant use is necessary. Consider using low-wattage bulbs, perhaps 25 watts, which require very little electricity.

353

> **Energy Tips**
>
> What do you think? Does it cost less to turn the lights off when leaving a room and turn them on again in ten minutes, or is it more econcmical to keep them on and prevent the surge of electricity needed to light them? Answer: It costs less to turn them off if the bulbs are incandescent, but it is more economical to leave them on if they are fluorescent lights and if you will return within a half-hour.

OTHER PRACTICAL ACCESSORIES

Screens. Screens can provide needed separation between parts of a room or mask an unattractive feature such as a radiator or an ugly view from a window. Inexpensive screens made of three, four, or five panels of wallboard hinged together can be purchased. The panels can be covered with paint, wallpaper, or fabric to match or contrast with the room. Or they can be covered with inexpensive posters, maps, and other paper decorations.

Wastebaskets and File Boxes. A wastebasket is a necessary and important accessory for many rooms. File and storage boxes may also be important accessories. Such file boxes are handy for storing recipes in the kitchen. In the study or bedroom, filing boxes can hold bills and schoolwork. And storage boxes are often used in the living room to hold game equipment or firewood. All of these useful objects can be made decorative.

Mirrors. In addition to its obvious use, a mirror can serve a design purpose by visually opening-up a room and making it seem larger. Mirrors should be sized in scale with the rest of a room's furnishings. A too-small mirror is useless; a too-large mirror gives a room an artificial, theatrical look. Mirrors can be bought ready-framed, of course. But if you happen to have or buy an old frame that is beautiful, you may prefer to have a mirror cut to fit it.

Clocks. A clock that keeps time accurately is a treasure in any room. When choosing a clock, however, be careful to listen closely to the sound of its ticking. And if the clock has chimes, listen to them, too. A clock's sounds should not be so loud that they will be distracting. In rooms where music is listened to, soundless

> **Energy Tips**
>
> Lamps with three-way switches and bulbs allow for low lighting levels when high illumination is unnecessary. Use the high switch only for reading and other activities which require close attention. Turn three-way bulbs down to the lowest level while watching television. There is less glare, and energy will be saved.

These bathroom mirrors can be used to create the illusion of depth and space in a small area.

electric clocks can be used. Obviously, you will want to be sure that the look of the clock harmonizes with the other objects in your room. Once in a while you may find an antique clock of such extraordinary beauty that its case alone might justify your buying and displaying it.

Pillows. Ready-made pillows can be bought in drapery departments and are sometimes expensive. If you cannot afford "decorator pillows," or if you find it difficult to locate ready-made pillows that harmonize with your room, you might like to make your own. You can either buy foam-rubber pillow forms or use retired, reshaped bed pillows. Cover them with fabric specifically chosen to blend in color and texture with the other objects in the room.

WALL TREATMENTS

Paintings have long been a favorite decoration for rooms. Many designers feel that nothing else can equal a fine painting as a focal point for a handsome interior design. If you love art, you should consider using paintings or good quality reproductions to decorate the rooms you design.

But paintings are only one kind of wall decoration. You can also use photographs, collages, posters, etchings, lithographs, maps, weavings, or fabric wall hangings. Your personal tastes and interests will determine which type of

---

Energy Tips

Many interesting effects have been produced by using mirrors to reflect light. One energy-saving effect is to mount a mirror on the wall at a right angle with a window so that sunlight will reflect from the mirror onto a darker wall or corner area. On occasions, this can substitute for light from a lamp.

355

Pillows add splashes of color and warmth to this sun room. They also harmonize with the upholstery of the day bed both in texture and shape. The rough-texture square pillows are more appropriate for an informal room.

wall decoration you choose. For the sake of convenience, we will use the single term *pictures* to include all of these possibilities. Never select a picture because it "picks up" the colors in your room! If you have already chosen it because it is a fine picture and it happens to have colors that are right in your room—fine! But never reverse the process!

Choosing A Frame

Pictures can be hung either framed or unframed. While very large pictures such as posters look quite attractive unframed, most pictures benefit from being framed.

First, consider the size of the picture to be framed. The smaller the picture, the narrower the frame should be. Larger pictures can accommodate wider frames.

Next, consider the color or tone of the frame. The frame's color should harmonize with the picture it surrounds. It should also harmonize with the other colors and tones used in the room.

Some artwork (photographs, drawings, etchings, and prints) look best when they are set off by *mats*. A mat is the heavy paperboard that separates the picture from the frame. A mat may be narrow or wide. It serves as a border between the frame and the picture. Mats are particularly effective on small pictures because mats help give such pictures more visual importance. Mats are also quite effective when the picture must hang against a patterned background, because they help separate the pictures from the background. Watercolors are

---

Energy Tips

Proper insulation is a necessity for reducing energy costs and waste. An attic with 15.4 centimeters (6 inches) of insulation will reduce heat loss by 12° on a sunny day.

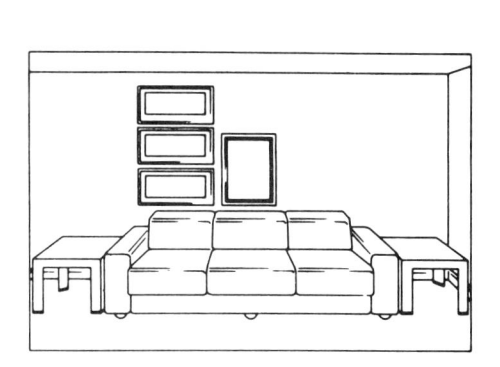

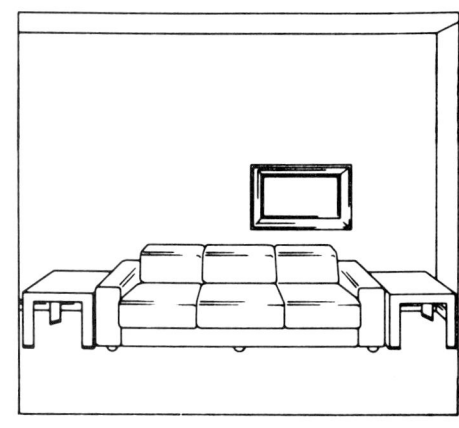

Place pictures in relationship to the furniture that they accompany. Possible placements include (top) informally balanced arrangements, (middle) a linear arrangement, (bottom left) a grouping, and (bottom right) a formally balanced arrangement.

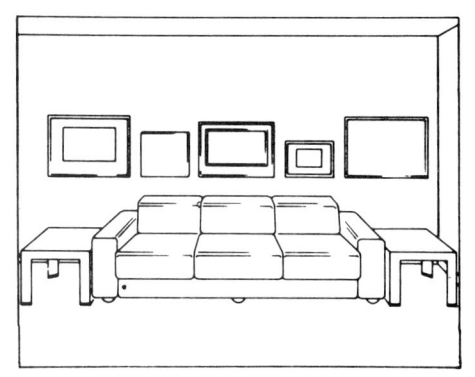

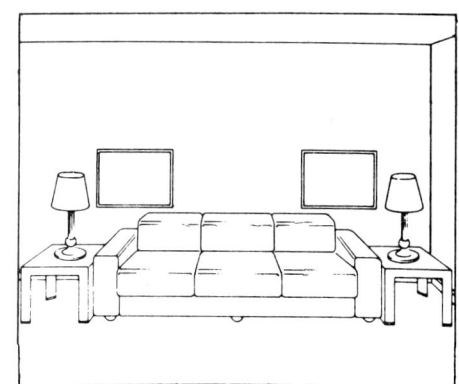

Energy Tips

If every gas-heated home were properly caulked and weatherstripped, we would save enough natural gas each year to heat close to 4 million homes.

always framed with a mat. On the other hand, mats are generally not used on oil paintings.

How to Hang Pictures

Once a picture has been framed to advantage, you want to be sure that you hang it to advantage. A properly hung picture is easily seen by people in the room. It relates in size and shape to the wall on which it hangs and to the pieces of furniture near which it hangs.

People have a tendency to hang pictures too high on a wall. Pictures should be hung at eye level. The height of eye level varies, depending on whether people in the room usually sit or stand. Pictures in a hallway should be hung for standing viewers, and pictures in a living room should be hung for seated viewers.

The safest procedure in deciding where on a wall to hang a picture follows: Cut a piece of paper the size and shape of the framed picture. Tape this piece of paper lightly to the wall in a test position. Then study it. Does it relate well to the furniture it hangs over or near? Does it seem balanced in its position. Or does it seem to "float" in space? While sitting in various parts of the room, can you gaze at the picture comfortably without craning your neck? Move the paper around until you are sure that you are happy with its placement. Only then are you ready to insert the picture hook into the wall.

Hanging Pictures in Groups

A single picture hanging by itself is often quite effective. But a room in which all the pictures are hung singly can look a bit boring. Avoid the monotony of placing one picture above each piece of furniture or one on each wall space. Instead, work toward variety in hanging pictures. Place one big picture on one

To plan a grouping of pictures, place a piece of paper on the floor and outline the grouping. Then check total effect and adjust. Attach the paper to the wall, pound in nails, and hang the pictures before removing paper.

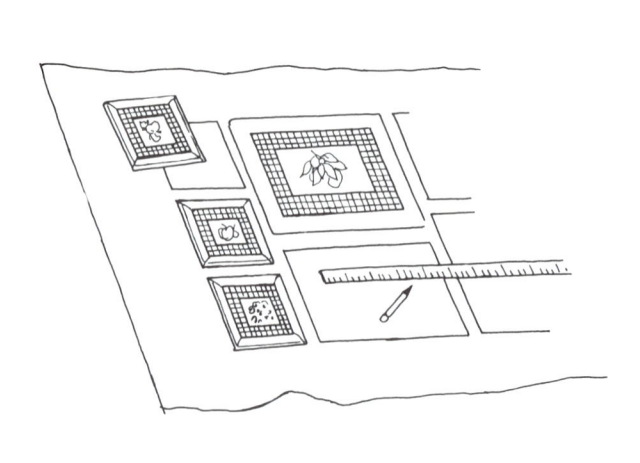

Hobbies, such as designing macrame wall hangings, have wonderful decorative possibilities. What hobby could you include in your room design?

wall, a grouping of two or three on another, and possibly a large grouping of quite a few smaller ones on still another. Do not overlook the possibility of combining pictures with objects of art mounted on brackets.

When pictures are grouped in relation to a piece of furniture, they need to be balanced. If the furniture is arranged for formal balance, the pictures should be hung in formal balance. For example, if a sofa is flanked by twin end tables, each supporting an identical lamp, the picture grouping over the sofa should be formally balanced, too. You might use a pair of identically shaped and sized pictures hanging side by side. Or you might use one larger picture centered over the sofa with a smaller pair of pictures hung on either side of the large one.

Informally balanced arrangements of furniture should, by the same token, be complemented by pictures informally balanced. For instance, a large picture hung over one end of a sofa. Groupings of smaller pictures need not be formally arranged.

A larger number of nonmatching pictures can be massed on a single "gallery" wall. You can harmonize such a grouping by keeping all the pictures within an imaginary rectangular outline.

Three-Dimensional Wall Decor

Pictures are the main choice of today's designers for wall decor, but they are not the only possibility. A beautiful three-dimensional object can be very exciting when hung on a wall either by itself or combined with a grouping of pictures. Folk masks from foreign countries and beautifully carved and costumed marionettes are two kinds of three-dimensional objects that designers have used for wall decor. Small wooden cabinets and plants hung from wall brackets are other popular wall accessories.

OTHER DECORATIVE ACCESSORIES

There are a number of objects you can add to a room that will not only enhance its overall appeal but will also help express your individuality. You should not regard a room design as finished until your have put your personal stamp on it. You can put your visual autograph on a room by means of one or more of the following accessories.

Hobby Collections

The United States is a nation of collectors. We collect everything from stamps and postcards to beer cans and antique Chinese porcelain. What do you collect? If your hobby has decorative possibilities, consider displaying at least part of your collection as an accessory to your room design. Several framed groupings of beautiful postage stamps hung prominently on a wall or a collection of seashells arranged artfully on a shelf would be an asset to almost any room.

Or, perhaps your collection is one of photos and clippings about some favorite television personality or recording star. A collage of such items, pasted decoratively to the panels of a screen and then covered with a thin coat of protective shellac, would add visual interest to a corner of your bedroom.

Objects of Art

Any room you design should have in it at least one beautiful object that will take your mind into imaginary realms far removed from the routine of your everyday world. It may be a beautiful piece of driftwood or a seashell you picked up on vacation. It may be a curio you bought as a souvenir of an exciting trip. It may be a treasured item given to you as a gift by a loved person or simply an object you bought for yourself because you found it too beautiful to resist. By using such an object as an accessory on a table top, a shelf, or a desk, you can put your personal mark on the room.

Plants and Flowers

Many people enjoy "bringing the outdoors inside" by using plants as accessories in the rooms they design.

To use plants effectively, however, you must understand the life demands of the plants you choose. Some plants can live and flourish only in bright, direct sunlight. Others do well in indirect light. Still others such as philodendron plants seem to flourish under almost any light condition. The amount of *humidity* (moisture) in a room is an important consideration, too. Before you acquire a plant for indoor use, then, learn enough about its needs to be sure that it has a fair chance of surviving in your room.

Flowers, of course, can add a great deal of excitement and zip to the look of a room. Because they perish so quickly, flowers are used only occasionally. You can either cut them from your own garden or purchase them at a florist's shop.

Dried flower arrangements can perk up a room. They have the added advantage of not needing any care. What other decorating possibilities are suggested by the world of plants and flowers?

During the winter, you can cut bare branches and arrange them in vases. The branches will create a lovely pattern and add some visual drama to your room.

What about using artificial plants and flowers? Many designers disagree on this point. Some say that if they cannot use real greenery, they will use none. Other designers have come to appreciate great improvements made in the quality of artificial plants and flowers in recent years. These designers sometimes use artificial greens, provided their quality is high. Of course, good artificial greens are expensive. But if you like them, use them.

This chapter has listed the main kinds of objects that designers use to accessorize their rooms. But it is important that you understand that the list is far from complete. The fact is, *anything* in a room—a magazine left open on an end table, a record jacket sitting on top of the stereo, a coffee cup set down on a table, even mail or schoolwork left on a desk—is an accessory as long as it remains in the room. Therefore, you do not have to choose every accessory for your room all at once. Accessories change as you change. The key is to choose a few important accessories first. The rest will be acquired naturally, as part of your living. If all of them reflect at least a part of your life and personality, it is likely they will look "at home" in any room you have designed.

Careers

A *buyer* purchases merchandise from a manufacturer or a wholesaler in expectation of meeting popular demand at the retail store where the buyer is employed. This involves skill in negotiating a good price, in determining the appropriate quantity to buy, and in showing an awareness of the latest trends. A buyer in the home-furnishings department may specialize in china, glassware, furniture, lighting, or floor or wall coverings.

Some of the duties of the job are planning purchases with a store's general manager; supervising the sales department; or working as an independent specialist, depending on the size and policy of the store. The job involves working with business managers, knowing customer tastes, and traveling to factories and showrooms. It takes quick judgment and aggressiveness to be a successful buyer.

A high school diploma is necessary, and college is helpful. Many institutions have training programs. Courses in math, sales, English, home economics, marketing, typing, and distributive education are some of the main ingredients.

Entry-level jobs are in the inventory or sales departments of large stores. A person might advance to head of the stock department and then to assistant buyer.

This career calls for an energetic, venturesome, analytical person who gets along with people and who has good business judgment. Overtime and willingness to work hard and take risks are part of the dynamic atmosphere. The pay is often excellent, depending on the size of the store.

Learning Experiences

1. Imagine that you are decorating a living room with a certain look. It could be provincial, dramatic, eclectic, contemporary, or traditional. Clip photographs or make sketches of at least five accessories that you think would be suitable for each room. (If the pictures are in color, be sure that their colors harmonize with one another.)
2. Study color photographs of designer rooms in magazines. Prepare a bulletin-board display showing unrealistic tricks and gimmicks that are used to make the accessories in the photograph "tie the design together." For example, are fresh flowers that are of a major color element in the design prominently displayed?
3. What interesting but unconventional accessory items could you use in a room to perform the functions of the following objects: bookends, paperweights, ash trays, vases, wastebaskets, candle holders, magazine holders?
4. Using objects brought from home, arrange a "still life" of accessories showing how several items can be attractively grouped on a tabletop to make an artistic statement.
5. Find a magazine illustration of a room with attractive accessories. Use examples or pictures to show how you could change the seasonal feel of the room through a change of accessories.

CHAPTER 9

Tableware and Household Linens

One of the most challenging and satisfying aspects of furnishing a home today is that there are so many opportunities to express your taste and your personality through the things you buy. There was a time when sheets, pillowcases, towels, and table linens were available only in shades of white. Dishes were bought in complete matching sets. *Flatware* (knives, forks, and spoons) was silver or plated silver and was also bought in complete matching sets. Choices of patterns and types of tableware were far more limited than they are today, too. That meant that buying tableware and household linens was a comparatively simple process. But it also meant that the process was not as much of a challenge or as much a source of pleasure as it can be today.

The wide range of color, design, and materials that manufacturers provide today ensures that you will be able to find tableware and household linen that suits your taste and your budget. But with so many possibilities from which to choose, how can you be sure that the decisions you make will prove the right ones?

In this chapter, we will first consider the broad subject of tableware. Essentially, that includes five different elements:

1. *Flatware* is the term for knives, forks, spoons, and related pieces used for serving and eating food.
2. *Dinnerware* refers to the plates, bowls, cups, and saucers from which we eat.
3. *Holloware* is the term for those food-serving pieces that hold quantities of food larger than a single portion. Pitchers, salad

363

Table settings can express the personality of the host or hostess.

bowls, and casserole dishes are examples of holloware. It is important to keep in mind, however, that the distinction between holloware and dinnerware is not always absolutely clear. Some sets of dinnerware include pieces of holloware. For example, some sets come with large serving bowls that match the plates and cups and that are included in the single purchase. In considering any piece for purchase, you need not worry too much about the category of the piece.

4. *Glassware* is the term used for beverage containers—whether they are made of glass or not. (An exception is the cup. Although it is a beverage container, it is considered dinnerware rather than glassware.)

5. *Table linen* is the term for all protective coverings placed on top of the dining table, regardless of the material of which they are made. Plastic place mats, lace doilies, and paper napkins are as much table linen as are linen napkins and tablecloths.

Energy Tips

When you use a dishwasher or a washing machine and dryer for tableware and household linens, try to schedule that use for nonpeak hours. Early in the morning and late in the evening are two good times.

Study tableware arrangements in stores for ideas before actually making your purchase.

FLATWARE

Silverware was the term once used for this category of table furnishings. That term, however, is far too limited now, because today we can choose from many possibilities other than pieces made of silver.

An entire piece of flatware may be made of one material. Or sometimes, the handle of a knife, fork, or spoon may be made of a material different from the part of the piece that actually comes in contact with food. The only important difference between the two types in terms of practicality is that flatware whose handles are made of a different material than their "working" parts may or may not be dishwasher-safe. It is essential, then, in buying flatware, to be certain whether or not the kind you are considering can be washed in a dishwasher. Price alone is not an indication. The fact that flatware is very expensive does not automatically ensure that it is dishwasher-safe. Expensive antique silver almost always includes knives that *cannot* be washed in a dishwasher. The blades of

Energy Tips

Running a dishwasher only when it is full is another good way to cut down on electric bills.

such knives are fastened to the handles with glues that will melt under the extremely high heat of today's dishwashers.

Sterling Silver

Sterling silver has always been regarded as the finest kind of flatware. The word *sterling* means the piece is made of high-quality, pure silver. Silver is a precious metal, so sterling silver flatware is very costly.

There are several reasons why sterling silver is a popular type of flatware. First, the more it is used, the more beautiful its finish becomes. Second, because sterling silver is a precious metal, a set of sterling flatware always retains some resale value. Other types of flatware simply become secondhand items after they are used. They retain little, if any, cash value in the marketplace. But sterling silver can usually be sold, if necessary, for a substantial amount of money. So many people regard the purchase of sterling flatware as an investment rather than as an expense. A third quality that makes sterling attractive is, quite simply, its snob appeal. Sterling silver is regarded as a status symbol.

On the other hand, there are two major drawbacks to sterling-silver flatware. The first, obviously, is its cost. With inflation, too, the cost goes higher every year. Related to this drawback is the question of whether to insure sterling silver. Because of its value, sterling silver is very attractive to thieves. The need to carry adequate insurance protection against such loss means an additional expense for owners of sterling. A second drawback to sterling silver is the fact that it tarnishes easily. Therefore, it must be polished regularly.

Silverplate

Less expensive than sterling silver is plated silver, or *silverplate*, or simply *plate,* as it is sometimes called. Flatware that is silverplated is made of a *base* (nonprecious) metal. This base metal is then given a covering of pure silver. The thickness of the covering is determined by the number of times the piece of flatware is dipped into its pure-silver bath. Double-plated flatware has two thin coverings of silver, one on top of the other. Triple-plated flatware has three such

This set of silverplated flatware complements the silver tea set. What disadvantages should be considered when buying silverplate?

Pewter flatware and glassware lend a note of elegance to the stoneware table setting.

coverings. Quadruple-plated flatware has four. Obviously, the more coverings of pure silver a piece has on it, the more expensive that piece will be.

In fine quality silverplate, tiny cubes of pure silver are imbedded at points where the piece is likely to wear the heaviest. The chief advantage of silverplated flatware is that is provides the look and beauty of sterling silver at a fraction of the cost. On the other hand, silverplate must be polished as frequently as sterling. The more you polish it, the more quickly you remove some of the thin silver covering on the piece's surface. When the silver covering is completely worn away from part of a piece, the piece is likely to look unattractive. It can then be *replated* (dipped into silver again), but this is an expensive process. You should carefully check the manufacturer's guarantee before you buy.

Stainless Steel

Much more popular today than either sterling or silverplate is flatware made of *stainless steel*. Stainless steel is made of a mixture of steel, nickel, and chromium. This mixture is virtually indestructible and does not tarnish with age or stain with use. When stainless-steel flatware was originally introduced in the marketplace, it was available only in a shiny finish and in light weight. It looked and felt cheap. Today, however, stainless-steel flatware is available in polished or satin finish and in handsome heavy weight.

Other Flatware Material

Gold-colored flatware is also available. This flatware is usually made of a solid metal alloy called *Dirylite*. Dirylite flatware tarnishes, but it holds its shine and color with considerably less care than silver. Because it is a solid metal, its finish will not wear off. So Dirylite flatware will last a lifetime. Because of its color, it goes especially well with dishes decorated with gold.

Also available is a wide variety of attractive flatware made with handles of china, wood, ivory, pearl, bone, and plastic. The knife blades, fork tines, and spoon bowls of such pieces are usually made of stainless steel.

Choosing Flatware Design

Regardless of the material of which flatware is made, you should carefully consider the flatware's *contour* (general shape) and weight. Some flatware that looks extremely attractive on a table is awkward to use and uncomfortable in the hand. For this reason, it is essential that you actually pick up the pieces and go through the motions of using them before you make a decision to buy. Knives, especially, should be tested. Does the knife handle allow you to grip the implement firmly, with no slipping? Is the relationship between the handle and the blade well balanced so that the knife will actually cut a piece of meat? Check spoons to be sure that the angle at which the bowl is placed in relation to the handle is one that will allow you to carry a full spoonful of liquid to your mouth without spilling half of it. Check forks to be sure that tines are deep enough to spear and hold a piece of food. Also be sure that the curve of the fork is adequate to hold a reasonable amount of food.

The next thing to consider is the visual appeal of the flatware. Whether you prefer plain, simple designs or more elaborate designs is a matter of personal taste. But you should always evaluate the look of a piece of flatware in terms of how its surface decoration relates to its silhouette. The area available for decoration on flatware is small. So it is important that any decoration on a piece relates harmoniously to the piece as a whole.

Finally, you will want to see how the flatware looks when placed with the dinnerware you are considering or that you already own. A flatware design that is beautiful in and of itself may look odd or out of place with a particular pattern of dinnerware. For instance, flatware with heavily curving contours and rich decoration of three-dimensional flowers looks odd if placed next to dinnerware that is decorated with a delicately patterned design. Simple flatware designs tend to look well with almost any dinnerware designs.

Shopping for Flatware

When you go shopping for flatware, follow the same rules as you would when shopping for any other home furnishings item. Put samples of each together and see what they do to each other. The price range in flatware is great. Comparison shopping is definitely worthwhile.

If you are considering buying either sterling, silverplate, or the higher quality stainless steel, there are some options you should know about that do not apply to the less-expensive types. In many cases, you can buy either by the piece

The unconventional design of contemporary flatware makes an attractive complement to the natural texture of woven straw placemats.

This place setting of stoneware and lucite and stainless-steel flatware is not very expensive. The relationship between the various elements is more important than their cost.

or by the *place setting* (a grouping of the four, five, or six different pieces of flatware necessary to serve a complete meal to one person). A place setting will include a fork, a knife, a soup spoon, and a teaspoon. It may also include a salad fork, a butter knife, or another piece.

If you buy by the place setting, you have the advantage of being able to use your flatware for some meals beginning with your first purchase. For example, if you start with two place settings, you can always use your flatware for dinners for two. Gradually, as you can afford to add to your set, you can purchase one place setting at a time.

If you buy by the piece, you have a different advantage. Under this system, you might buy, as your first purchase, six or eight teaspoons. These you could use whenever you entertained friends for tea or coffee. Later, you would add an appropriate number of forks, and then knives, and so on. Whenever you buy a partial set of flatware, be sure to check on whether the pattern you have chosen will be available from the manufacturer for a long time to come.

Mixing Patterns

If you know definitely that you prefer to mix patterns of flatware, you may consider shopping for silver and silverplate in antique shops. Occasionally, antique shops will have a complete set of matched silver available for purchase. But that requires a tremendous outlay of money all at once. However, it is not uncommon to "build" an entire set of antique silver by buying six knives here, six spoons there, six forks somewhere else. The patterns of silver bought this way will not match, but careful selection can ensure that they harmonize.

DINNERWARE

As with flatware, dinnerware is available today in a fantastic array of materials, quality, designs, colors, and prices. Dinnerware historically was made in such durable materials as silver, pewter, and wood. But to most people, the term *dinnerware* means objects made of a ceramic material. Ceramic dinnerware was first manufactured in China. To this day, all dinnerware, regardless of where it is made, is sometimes referred to as "china."

Fine china has heirloom qualities. It is beautiful, highly durable, and quite expensive.

Chinaware

Actually, only dinnerware made of the finest white clay is correctly called chinaware. This clay, when *fired* (baked in a special oven called a *kiln*) at an extremely high temperature, becomes semitranslucent. That is, when the object is held so that a light source is behind it, a small amount of light can actually be seen through it. Such china is durable, chip-resistant, and nonporous. It gives off a bell-like tone when tapped. Nonporous china has a surface so smooth that no trace of liquid can seep into it.

A special variety of chinaware is *bone china*. To make bone china, manufacturers mix the white clay with finely crushed animal bone. Bone china is usually extremely thin and chip resistant.

Another word for any fine china is *porcelain*. The name *porcelain* comes from the Italian word for a kind of pearl shell that has the same exquisite whiteness and sheen of this china. Porcelain, bone china, and all fine china are to dinnerware what sterling silver is to flatware. They are the most expensive and most valuable dinnerware that you can buy.

Earthenware

When coarser clay is shaped into dinnerware pieces that are slightly heavier in weight and fired at lower temperature than chinaware, the product is called *earthenware*. Earthenware is *opaque*; that is, no light can pass through it. Earthenware is also somewhat porous. Traces of liquid seep beneath the surface into tiny spaces in the clay body of the dinnerware. Eventually, this leads to visible discoloration. Earthenware is more likely to chip and crack than china. When struck, it gives off a flatter, duller tone than porcelain.

A much coarser clay, formed into considerably heavier shapes than earthenware and fired at a still lower temperature, is called *pottery*. Pottery is highly susceptible to chipping and breaking. Also, pottery's finish is apt to be somewhat rough and quite porous, even after it has been *glazed* (covered with a smooth surface). Because of its comparatively crude look, pottery is charmingly informal. It looks very much at home in casual and provincial settings. Italy, Mexico, Portugal, and China all export pottery to the United States. Much of it is beautifully designed and gaily colorful. If you buy hand-painted pottery, however, it is extremely important that you determine whether it is safe for table use. There have been tragic cases in which acids in food dissolved the paint with which some pottery has been painted. The dissolved paint then poisoned people eating from the dishes. If you are not absolutely sure that hand-painted pottery is safe, ask before you buy.

Plastic Dinnerware

Plastic dinnerware is now available in a wide range of shapes and styles. Generally made of melamine, it is especially popular in homes where children help with the dishes because it is virtually indestructible. Most plastic dinnerware can withstand the high temperature of dishwashers. Although it will not break, it can be cracked by dropping. It can also be scratched and stained through normal use. However, the cost of plastic dinnerware is so low compared with the cost of ceramic dinnerware that many people choose it. These people accept the fact that they may have to replace it within a few years when its appearance has deteriorated.

Almost all dinnerware available today will adequately serve the purpose for which it is intended. So consideration of its design is primarily a matter of personal preference and budget.

Decoration

Before looking at the surface decoration of dinnerware, look at the pieces in silhouette. Does the shape or outline of the cups and soup bowls please you? Do cup handles seem a well-balanced element in the overall shape of the cup? Or do they look as though they were pasted on as a sort of afterthought? Do you prefer plates that are almost flat in outline? Or do you prefer those that have a defined center with an edge or rim to hold while serving?

By now, you have learned how to judge surface decoration in general. Therefore, we do not need to discuss it in detail once more. But there are two special considerations to keep in mind when judging the surface decoration of dinnerware. First, it is important to visualize how the dinnerware will look with

China, stoneware, and pottery dinnerware range from the traditional to the modern. The variety of styles, shapes, colors, and decoration is dazzling.

food on it. Many patterns that are beautiful in and of themselves are too complicated to look good with food. Some colors do not blend with food successfully. For example, a bright green may make cooked green vegetables look dull and unappetizing by contrast. Some reds look unattractive with meat. So, while evaluating the decoration of dinnerware, keep in mind the foods that you will serve.

Second, be sure to find out whether the decoration is dishwasher-safe. If the dinnerware has gold decoration applied by hand, that decoration could discolor or wash off entirely in the extremely hot water used in dishwashers.

Buying Dinnerware

As with flatware, some people prefer all of their dinnerware to match. Others prefer to use several different patterns, harmonized with each other by related color or design schemes. Glass, metal, or wooden bowls or plates are often added as accent pieces. The approach you choose will depend on your personal taste.

Almost all good dinnerware on the market today can either be bought in place settings of a minimum number of pieces or from *open stock* (piece by piece). Fortunately, the better the dinnerware, the more likely it is that the manufacturer will continue to make it in years to come. This means that additions and replacements to your dinnerware will be possible. To be on the safe side, however, it is always a good idea to buy a few extra cups and large plates in the pattern you have chosen, since cups and plates are the pieces that most often must be replaced.

Occasionally, you can make an extremely good buy on dinnerware when you purchase it in a complete, preassembled set. Sometimes, such sets are even offered at special rates by banks, supermarkets, and other merchants to attract new customers. The one thing to keep in mind if you take advantage of such an offer is that it will be almost impossible to replace or add matching pieces once the special offer has expired.

Finally, before you choose your dinnerware, test its appearance with the flatware you own or are thinking of buying. This will help you avoid choosing flatware and dinnerware that do not complement each other.

HOLLOWARE

Holloware, you will recall, refers to serving pieces. Bowls, tureens, pitchers, and casseroles are typical holloware pieces. Often, such pieces can be bought to match your dinnerware. However, more and more people are tending to choose their holloware separately from their dinnerware. This gives some variety to the look of a completely set table. Also, some new types of holloware are particularly useful in a way that holloware in dinnerware material is not.

There are available today a wide range of serving pieces designed to go from freezer to oven to table. Use of such pieces saves time in meal preparation and saves space in the dishwasher when it is time for after-meal cleanup. Some serving pieces are designed in two parts. One part is a food container that can go into the oven. The other part is a decorative frame into which the food container can be placed before it is brought to the table. Some pieces have a built-in heating element to maintain the temperature of cooked food at the table.

Holloware pieces are made of many materials that we have already discussed such as silver, stainless steel, ceramics, and plastics. Glass is another popular choice for many holloware pieces, especially those which will not hold hot food. Wood is popular, too, particularly for salad bowls. But wooden pieces will not withstand washing in a dishwasher; they must be washed by hand.

The chief consideration in choosing holloware is the function the piece is intended to serve. Once you have decided that the piece will perform well, you should consider the amount of storage space it will require. Of course, you should also evaluate the piece's appearance in relation to the dinnerware and flatware with which it will be used.

GLASSWARE

Beautiful glassware is an asset to any table. It adds height, sparkle, and variety to a table setting. When beautiful glassware blends harmoniously with the dinnerware and flatware, it adds enormously to a table's attractiveness.

Glassware is available in a wide range of qualities, styles, and prices. Like dinnerware, glassware presents the problem of breakage. Much glassware is available in the same pattern over a period of many years, however, so replacement is possible. Glassware generally costs less than dinnerware, so replacing an entire set from time to time is usually not a financial burden.

Glasses divide according to overall shape into stemware, footed tumblers, and tumblers.

Glassware is generally divided into three basic shapes. *Stemware* is the most elegant of glassware. In silhouette, stemware shows the *bowl* of the glass (the part that holds the liquid) perched on a tall *stem* (or column). The stem is fastened to a flat base. *Footed tumblers* have the bowl of the glass fastened directly to the base. *Plain tumblers* are glasses with no separate base. Even in completely matched sets of glassware (which are not as fashionable now as they once were), more than one shape of glass may be represented.

Buying Glassware

To ensure that the glassware you choose will harmonize with your dinnerware and flatware, you should try to actually place examples of each side by side. You will also want to consider the kind of use your glassware will get. Fragile, delicate stemware is not likely to last long in a home where meals and after-meal cleanup are usually rushed and frantic. Expensive glassware is not likely to be a sensible choice in a home with little children who have difficulty wrapping their small hands around glasses. You should also take into account such practical matters as storage and dishwasher capacity. If you are short on cupboard space, one or two basic sizes of glassware may meet all your beverage-serving needs effectively.

TABLE LINEN

The range of table linens available today is tremendous. Generally, however, table linens can be divided into three categories: tablecloths, place-mats, and napkins.

Tablecloths

A tablecloth should usually be large enough to cover the entire table and hang over the edge by about 15 to 18 centimeters (6 to 7 inches) all around. Tablecloths are available in round, oval, and rectangular shapes, in a wide range of sizes. For formal dining, tablecloths have always been considered essential. But since few of us today live or entertain formally, tablecloths are far less popular than they once were. This is particularly true of tablecloths made of such fabrics as linen and lace, which require very careful laundering and ironing.

Fortunately, tablecloths are now available in wrinkle-resistant, drip-dry, and permanent-press fabrics. This means that people who enjoy using tablecloths need not become slaves to their upkeep. Of course, for very informal dining, there are tablecloths made of sturdy plastic-coated or all-plastic fabrics. Such tablecloths can be easily cleaned with a damp sponge.

People who like cloth table coverings but who are unwilling to devote the time necessary to constant washing and ironing often choose a *runner*. A runner is a narrow strip of fabric, usually about 36 centimeters (14 inches) wide, placed down the middle of a table. Individual place settings are put directly on the polished wood of the table. Because the runner does not come into direct contact with diners' plates and glasses, it remains clean through many meals. Therefore, it does not need to be changed or laundered with the same frequency as a full tablecloth.

A champagne-beige, lace-trimmed linen tablecloth creates an elegant background for this formal table setting.

Placemats

Individual placemats are an increasingly popular choice of today's homemakers. Placemats may be rectangular, round, oval, or wedge-shaped. They are usually approximately 28 centimeters by 43 centimeters (11 inches by 17 inches). The variety of materials of which placemats are made includes all sorts of fabrics, as well as plastic. Very attractive placemats made of composition board and decorated with prints are also available.

A chief attraction of placemats is that their use makes it fairly easy to maintain a high level of cleanliness with little effort. A soiled mat can be wiped clean or replaced by a fresh one, leaving the entire table setting spotless once again. Another advantage of placemats is that they come in sizes appropriate to all sizes and shapes of tables. A third advantage is that placemats are available in a wide range of prices.

Napkins

There was a time when linen napkins were the only kind available. Today, they are still in demand for the most formal and elegant dining situations. But a variety of less-expensive, more-easily-cared-for fabric napkins are now available in all conceivable colors and designs and textures. Of course, paper napkins have replaced cloth napkins in many homes—and with good reason. Paper napkins are inexpensive, save labor, and make it possible to have napkins that are absolutely clean at each meal. On the other hand, people concerned with our nation's ecology problems point out that paper napkins are wasteful of our natural resources. Such people recommend using easy-care drip-dry napkins, which can be washed and dried with a minimum of effort.

The proper placement of tableware has both practical and aesthetic value. Each piece of flatware, glassware, and china is in a position that makes its use comfortable and natural; and the accurately repeated pattern at each place is beautiful and satisfying.

TABLE SETTINGS

Setting a table attractively is like composing a picture. With a bit of care and effort, the result can be made to look attractive and inviting.

The placement of flatware on a table has long been determined by custom and tradition. Generally speaking, it is arranged according to the order in which it is used. Pieces to be used for the first course are placed at the outer edges of the arrangement. The forks are placed at the left of the place setting. Knives and spoons are placed on the right. (An easy way to remember this is that the word *fork* and the word *left* have the same number of letters. The words *spoon* and *knife* and the word *right* have the same number of letters.) Glasses are usually placed above the tip of the knife. Napkins may be placed on the plate, under the fork, or to the left of the fork. Each piece of flatware, glassware, and dinnerware should be in a position that makes its use comfortable and natural.

Modern living is so rushed that it is often impractical to have a decorative accent on the table at every meal. But when you have time to add such an accent, it can make the table more attractive and inviting. The decoration may be placed in the center of the table or at one end. Flowers are perhaps the favorite accent. But there are many other possibilities for an attractive centerpiece. A potted plant, a basket or bowl of fruit or vegetables, or even a newly baked and frosted cake can be a delightful decoration. An art object or a grouping of natural objects, such as a bowl of pine cones, can be lovely as a centerpiece. Candles are another popular choice as a decorative table accent. The single thing to remember in choosing a table decoration is that it should not be so high that it prevents diners from seeing each other across the table. It should also not be so wide that it crowds the placement of serving dishes on the table.

HOUSEHOLD LINEN

The term *household linen* includes bed linen, bath linen, and kitchen linen. (As in the case of the term *table linen,* the objects need not be made of linen to fall into the household linen category.) The range of household linen available today is remarkable in terms of quality, color, design, and price.

Bed Linen

Sheets and pillowcases represent a major expense to the first-time homemaker. A general rule of thumb to apply in deciding how many of each you need is to multiply the number of beds and pillows by three. This will enable you to have one set of linen in use, one in the laundry, and one lying clean in the cupboard or closet.

Cotton is now the most popular fabric for bed linen. The highest quality of cotton sheeting is percale. It is the lightest to handle and to iron, and it feels silky smooth. Thread counts, which tell the total number of crosswise and lengthwise threads in a square inch of fabric, approximate 180 to 200 per square inch in percale.

Muslin is a less expensive kind of cotton sheeting. It has a thread count of 112, 128, or 140 per square inch. Muslin is heavier to handle than percale, and it wrinkles more easily. It is also rougher to the touch. (Unfortunately, manufacturers sometimes fill muslin with a starchy substance to make it look and feel smoother and more-closely woven than it is. But that substance disappears with the first washing, leaving the fabric limp and lifeless.) On the other hand, an advantage of muslin over percale is muslin's greater durability.

The bold, colorful pattern of these coordinated sheets, pillowcases, and comforter add a vital design element to this contemporary bedroom.

A harmony of design is created by matching the floral fabric of quilts and cafe curtains in this Early American style bedroom.

Polyester, a synthetic fiber, is sometimes combined with cotton to produce a sheeting material that has an extradurable finish that is wrinkle-resistant. Such fabric feels rougher to the touch than percale. *Rayon,* another synthetic, may be combined with cotton to produce a fabric that is smooth to the touch. Rayon-and-cotton bed linen often proves unsatisfactory, however, because it is so slippery that sheets made of it keep slipping off the bed and onto the floor.

Sheets and Pillowcases. Sheets are available in both flat and *fitted* (or contoured) styles. A fitted bottom sheet has four corners that are sewn so that they slip over the mattress and hold the sheet firmly in place. Fitted sheets make sleep more comfortable because the sheet remains taut. On the other hand, fitted sheets are harder to iron, fold, and store.

Flat sheets are generally bought in a size 61 centimeters (24 inches) wider and 61 centimeters (24 inches) longer than the mattress size. This extra fabric allows them to be firmly tucked in under the mattress. See the chart on page 380 for an indication of the different standard sizes in which sheets are generally available.

Pillowcases are generally bought slightly wider than the pillow itself, and from 15 centimeters (6 inches) to 25 centimeters (10 inches) longer than the pillow. The three basic sizes of pillows are the standard, the queen size, and the king size. Be certain you know which size your pillows are before shopping for pillowcases. Also available on the market today are zippered protector cases. These are meant to be slipped over the pillow itself and zipped up. The zippered case is then covered with a regular pillowcase. Such zippered protector cases lengthen the life of the pillow. These cases also help to prevent the *ticking* (the fabric cover) of the pillow from becoming soiled.

Blankets. Whether you choose blankets, comforters, or quilts for your beds will depend upon climate, allergies, and personal preference. (Some people like the greatest warmth with the least weight, while others sleep soundly only if the bed covering feels heavy to them.)

Wool blankets are considered by many to be the finest type of warm bed covering available. They provide warmth without too much weight, and they are very durable. On the other hand, wool blankets must be specially treated in washing or dry cleaning to prevent shrinking and matting.

Cotton blankets are a choice for summer or for climates where a great deal of night warmth is not necessary. One special kind of cotton blanket is the *sheet blanket*. This is a very thin bed covering that is just a bit heavier than a bed sheet. Another special kind of cotton blanket is the *thermal blanket*. The thermal blanket has a mesh weave that contains may air holes which hold body heat. When covered with a nonmesh fabric such as a sheet, a thermal blanket produces the warmth of a much heavier blanket.

Manufactured fibers have taken a large place in the blanket market because of their easy care. When used separately or blended together and napped heavily, acrylics, modacrylics, rayon, and nylon hold much warmth and are light in weight. The acrylics are especially noted for their washability.

Yet another very popular kind of blanket is the electric blanket. The thermostatic controls on such blankets allow for a complete range of heat with no change of bedding. Electric blankets are also quite lightweight. Double-sized electric blankets are often equipped with dual controls. This allows two persons sharing a bed to meet their individual needs for heat without inconveniencing each other. Although electric blankets require special care in cleaning, you need have no fear about safety involved in using one. Electric blankets are completely safe, unless they have been damaged, of course. On the other hand, those who are concerned about conserving fuel prefer not to use these fuel-consuming blankets.

Comforters and Quilts. Unlike blankets, comforters and quilts are not made of a single kind of fabric. Instead, they consist of a fabric case inside of which is sandwiched a layer of filling. The filled case is then either tied or quilted (stitched in an all-over pattern) to keep the filling evenly distributed. A quilt is thinner than a comforter. It frequently serves the dual purpose of bed cover and bedspread in provincial rooms. Historically, quilt cases were homemade, with covers of patchwork or appliquéd fabric. Today, most quilts are machine-made, but they are often designed in imitation of the homemade variety.

Cotton-sateen, rayon, acetate, or silk cases, when filled with down, feathers, wool, or synthetic-fiber fillings, make puffy, light-weight comforters. Cotton filling is occasionally used, but it often becomes lumpy with use. In buying comforters or quilts, be sure to consider any personal allergies which might make certain types of filling a health problem.

HOUSEHOLD LINEN

TABLE LINEN

Tablecloths
Full size: extend 6″ below edge of table
Stock sizes:
  36 by 54 inches   54 by 54 inches   72 by 90 inches
  45 by 54 inches   64 by 72 inches   90 by 108 inches
Place mats: stock size, 11 by 17 inches
Breakfast cloths   Bridge table covers

Napkins
Fabric, stock sizes:
  dinner: 24 by 24 inches
  breakfast: 18 by 18 inches
  luncheon: 15 by 15 inches
  tea: 12 by 12 inches
  cocktail: 7 by 7 or 5 by 8 inches
Paper — to save work — for family meals

Fabrics
Damask: widths — 36, 42, 54, 58, 64, 72, 80, 90 inches
Pure linen is 95 percent linen — frequently blended with cotton
Part linen is 25 percent linen plus cotton
Manmade fibers in various weaves are used for place mats
Lace used for tablecloths and place mats is made from linen, cotton, nylon and other manmade fibers

Quantity
Tablecloth: 1 — linen, lace, damask
Place mats: 2 sets — fabric or plastic with napkins
Breakfast cloths: 2, with napkins unless paper preferred
Dinner napkins: 6 to 12, depending on quantity of other tableware

BATHROOM

Towels and washcloths
Stock sizes:
  Bath towels: 24 by 28 and 40 by 52 inches
  Face towels: 16 by 26 and 18 by 36 inches
  Washcloths: 12 by 12 inches

Preferred fabric
Cotton terry cloth — firmly woven edges, fluffy loops
Huck toweling — preferred by some for face towels

Quantity
Bath towels: 4 per person
Washcloths: 4 per person
Face towels: 4 per person

Bathmats
22 by 36 inches in heavy terry cloth, or manmade fibers in a pile weave
At least 2 per bathroom

BED LINEN

Sheets
Flat: 24 inches wider and 24 inches longer than mattress
Fitted: tight but not enough to buckle mattress
Sizes: (all quoted torn and unshrunk — finished size 10 inches less)
  Crib: 45 by 77 inches
  Twin: 72 by 108 to 113 inches
  Double: 90 by 108 to 113 inches
  King: 108 by 120 inches
  Extra length: all 120 inches long

Pillow cases
Standard measurement: 2 to 3 inches wider and 10 inches longer than pillow
Standard size: 21 by 27 inches

Blankets
Standard measurement: 10 inches longer and 18 inches wider than mattress
Standard sizes Twin: 65 by 90 inches
                Double: 80 by 90 inches
                King: 90 by 108 inches

Preferred fabrics
Cotton
  Muslin: heavy yarns — thread count per square inch: 112-140
  Percale: fine yarns — thread count per square inch: 180-200
  Blend: nylon and percale — wrinkle-free, no iron
  Knitted: cotton and blend — preferred for crib
Wool: warmest, most expensive, used for blankets
Acrilon-Orlon blends: warm, mothproof, shrink and felt resistant, excellent for blankets
Cotton: used for summer blankets

Quantity
Sheets: 4 per bed (6 better)
Pillow cases: 2 per pillow (3 better)
Blankets: 2 per bed
Spreads: 1 per bed

KITCHEN LINENS

Towels
Preferred size: 18 by 30 inches
Preferred fabric:
  Linen or part linen for glassware
  Bleached cotton
Quantity: 6 to 12

Other kitchen linens
3 knit or terry cloth dishcloths, stock size: 12 by 12 inches
4 quilted or terry cloth pot holders, stock size: 5 by 5 inches

Buying Bed Linen. All bed linen is available in an almost infinite range of colors and patterns. Choosing bed linens that will harmonize with or provide a contrasting accent to the rest of the room's decor is not difficult. Simply let yourself be guided by the principles you have been reading about in this book. There is no reason to choose only matching linens. Different sets of sheets and pillowcases and blankets can add constant variety to a bedroom.

On the other hand, it is only practical to choose all of the linen for a given bedroom in such a way that the items relate to each other. For example, suppose you are choosing linen for a bedroom whose primary color is blue. You might choose the following assortment:

Bottom Sheet	Top Sheet	Pillow Case
Solid pale blue Dark- and light-blue stripes on white Solid white	Solid pale blue Dark- and light-blue stripes on white Floral in several blues	Solid pale blue Solid white Floral in several blues

Such an assortment would give you a large number of different "mix-and-match" possibilities. It would also ensure that when a single item became torn or worn, you could still use the remaining items in combination. Three different

Shower curtains are an important decorative element in today's bathrooms. They are available in an array of styles, fabrics, colors, and patterns. Notice how the colorful, striped pattern of this shower curtain in picked up again in the toilet-seat cover and the window shade.

sets of bed linen in three different color combinations would not allow you to practice this economy.

Bath Linen

In choosing towels, the main qualities to consider are their durability and *absorbency* (ability to soak up and hold moisture). Face cloths, bath towels, and hand towels are usually made of cotton *terry cloth,* also called *Turkish toweling.* This is a type of fabric in which uncut loops of fiber cover the surface of the towel, giving it a rough, nubby texture. If the fabric is densely woven, the loops are less liable to wear thin or pull out. To judge the comparative firmness of different towelings, check the *selvage* (the hem), where there are no loops. You can readily see how tightly or loosely woven the cloth is.

Occasionally, people like to add a special, finer kind of towel to their assortment of bath linens. These towels are called *guest towels,* or *fingertip towels.* Such towels are generally more delicate than terry-cloth towels. They are frequently made of fine fabrics such as linen and decorated with embroidery. Of course, they require much more care in laundering and ironing than terry-cloth towels do. But homemakers feel the effort is justified.

The other basic item of bath linen is the shower curtain. Many people choose a shower curtain made of easy-care plastic. But interior designers often prefer to use a double shower curtain. The inner curtain, called the *liner,* is made of plain plastic. The outer curtain which never comes in contact with water is generally made of the same fabric as the bathroom curtains. A double curtain is, of course, more expensive than a single plastic shower curtain. However, many designers feel that the extra expense is justified by the added elegance the double curtain usually gives a bathroom.

Buying Bath Linen. Choosing the colors and patterns of your bath linen is an exercise in matching colors. The reason is that most bathrooms have at least part of their wall surface covered with permanently colored tiles. Finding bath linen to match or harmonize with the tiles in your present bathroom should not be too great a problem. But what if you move and the tiles in your new bathroom are a different color? Your selection of bath linen may clash with the color in that new bathroom. The only sure way to avoid this problem is to choose bath linen in white. Most of us, however, would hate to rule out buying bath linens in some of the lovely patterns and colors that are available. You might compromise. Select large, high-quality bath towels in white or beige. Then, select hand towels or washcloths in a color or pattern to add some visual interest and variety to your present bathroom. The large towels would be likely to harmonize with whatever colors happened to be in the bathroom of your next home.

Kitchen Linen

Changing housekeeping techniques have meant that today's kitchens need fewer linens than were needed in the past. For example, many people no longer dry dishes regularly by hand. They either dry them in the dishwasher or let them air-dry in the kitchen drainboard. The result is that most people no longer require dozens of dish towels. Similarly, the use of sponges and pot-scrubbing pads has eliminated the need for many dishcloths.

Pots and pans, bulky serving dishes, and some glassware and flatware still occasionally need to be dried by hand. For this purpose, linen towels and cotton-huck towels are the most absorbent and the most lint-free. Many kitchen hand towels are now made of terry cloth. Disposable paper toweling is also popular.

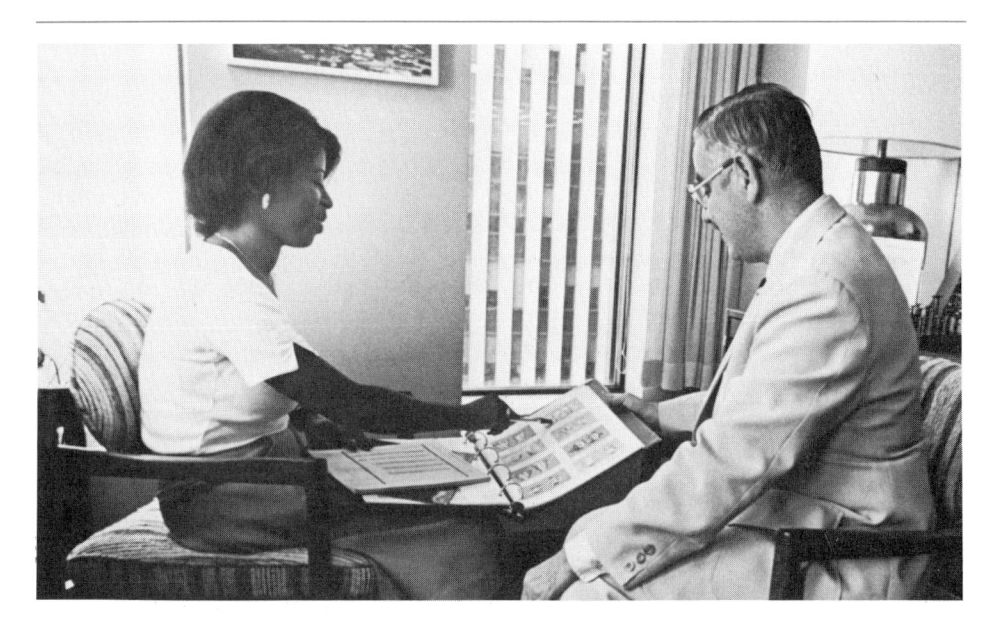

Careers

The manufacturer's representative sells to buyers from wholesale and retail companies. A "rep" must travel extensively and have a good sales ability. This job is one of the most highly paid sales positions. The representative must plan strategies and use appropriate techniques to sell to store buyers or executives in the purchasing department.

In order to sell in this job, one must understand the clients' needs, take initiative, have a good sense of timing, be aggressive, and offer appropriate and resourceful suggestions. Enthusiasm for the job comes from a sincere belief in the product.

Specialized knowledge or college training is required, in addition to completion of the company training program. The college courses that are recommended are home economics, business, economics, advertising, sociology, and psychology. One may easily gain some helpful experience through part-time work at Christmas and during the summer.

An ability to develop good relationships with customers, a well-groomed appearance, and the ability to take pressure are necessary personal qualifications. A manufacturer's representative has the opportunity for advancement to management positions.

Learning Experiences

1. Assemble a collage of photographs clipped from advertisements showing designs of dishes, flatware, glassware, placemats, and napkins that you think would harmonize for an attractive table setting.
2. Invite the buyer from the dinnerware department of a local department store to address your class on the variety of tableware available today. Topics might include how the buyer chooses items the store will stock and how consumer tastes have changed in the past twenty years.
3. Assume that you are choosing flatware and dishes for an individual or a family who will not have an everyday set plus a set for special occasions. This tableware will be used for all meals. Find patterns in magazine ads or through actual store visits that you think would work successfully under formal as well as informal circumstances.
4. Design a set of bed linen or a set of tableware in your favorite color scheme.
5. Bring to class an unusual, unconventional item that you think would make an appropriate table centerpiece for a dinner party. Explain how it would be arranged.

Index

accents, 230–231, 233, 281
accessories, 300, 348–361
acetate, 325
Acrilan, 326, 380
acrylics
    fibers, 326, 379
    floor coverings, 249, 253
    paints, 256
allergies, 290, 379
attics, insulation of, 356, 364
awning windows, 332

backgrounds, room design, 238–240, 249–269
bamboo curtains, 340–341
bath linen, 380, 382
bedding (bed linen), 377–382
bedrooms, 289, 300, 307
beds, 277, 283, 284, 285, 300
blankets, 300, 379, 380
bone china, 273, 370
bookcases, 273, 300
brass, decorative, 281
broadloom, 250, 252
brocade, 328
broilers, counter-top, 394, 422–424
brooms, electric, 479
budgets, 263, 265, 291, 300
butt joints, 294

careers
    buyer, home-furnishings, 361
    carpenter, 302
    extension worker, 269–270
    furniture finisher, 302
    furniture retailing, 302
    housekeeping management, 321–322
    interior designer, 218
    manufacturer's representative, 383
    photographer, 236–237
    shipping clerk, 302
    textile chemist, 347
    textile designer, 347
    upholsterer, 302
carpeting, 250–253, 264, 269
carving, 238, 275
casement cloth, 328
casement windows, 331–332
caulking, 357
ceiling treatments, 234, 238, 260–262, 263, 268, 350
chairs, 281, 284, 300
    comfort in, 278, 290, 297
chandeliers, 281, 350
charcoal, burning of, 310
chests, budget for, 300
chinaware, 300, 370
Chippendale, 272
chromium (chrome), 272, 282
climate, 213, 234
clocks, 354–355
Colonial-style furniture, 272, 273, 277
color, 220–236
    in linens, 381, 382
    in paint, 267
    in window treatments, 334
color schemes, 228–236
contemporary (modern) style, 281–282
corner blocks, 293, 295
cornices, window, 335
cotton, 253, 324, 325, 379
curtains, 268, 300, 326, 332–335, 342–346

damask, 273, 328, 380
desks, 277, 285
dinnerware, 300, 363, 364, 369–372
door frames, 262
dovetailing, 294, 295
dowels, 293–294, 295
drafts, protection from, 249, 259, 278, 346
drawers, 294, 295, 296
dry-cleaning, 325, 346

earthenware, 370–371
eighteenth-century furniture, 277, 278, 281
electric blankets, 379

fabrics, 323–329
    upholstery, 290, 296–297
    as wall coverings, 258, 259–260
fibers, 252–253, 323–328
fireplaces, 260, 310, 311
flatware, 363, 365–369, 376
floor coverings, 250–255, 264, 265, 267
    fibers for, 252–253, 325–326
flooring materials, 240, 249–250
floor plans, 263, 299, 303–306
fluorescent lights, 227, 335, 350, 354
food processors, 430–431
furniture
    antique, 275, 277, 299
    arrangement of, 287, 303–321
    construction of, 293–296
    finishes, 274–275, 286, 290, 294, 296
    money-saving, 285–287
    outdoor, 286–287, 326
    outlets for, 297–299, 301

385

period (traditional), 275–281
price and quality of, 292, 301
renovation of, 274
secondhand, 285–286, 299
space-saving, 215, 283–285
unfinished, 286
upholstered, 278, 282, 290, 296–297

gas, heating with, 357,
glass, 272, 282, 329
glassware, 300, 364, 373–374
grain (wood), 292, 293

hardware, 294, 346
heating economies, 224, 309, 311, 324, 356, 357
heat-resistant finish, 296
holloware, 363–364, 372–373
homespun, 327
horsehair upholstery, 281
houseplants, 335
huck toweling, 380
hues, 223, 224, 225, 226

insulation, heat
    buildings, 329, 356, 364
    furnishings and, 213, 249, 259, 324

jalousie windows, 332

kitchen equipment budget, 300
kitchens, 306

labels, fabric, 328, 329, 346
lamps, 300, 350–354
lampshades, 352

latex paints, 256
leather upholstery, 281, 290, 327
life-styles, design and, 212–216, 272–273, 277–278
light bulbs, 348, 352, 354
lighting
    economies in, 224, 348, 349, 352, 354, 355
    outdoor, 348
linen (fabric), 324–325, 327
    wall coverings, 258
linen, household, 300, 364, 377–383
linoleum, 250

mahogany, 273, 277, 281, 292–293
maintenance
    floor coverings, 265, 267
    floors, 240, 249
maple furniture, 277, 292
matchstick curtains, 340–341
mats (picture), 236, 356, 358
mattresses, 291, 300
mildew, 253, 267
mirrors, 300, 354, 355
modacrylics, 253, 326, 379
modular furniture, 282, 284–285
moldings, 262, 263
mood (design and), 234, 239, 287
moving, 213–214, 216–217
muslin, 377, 380

nails (in furniture), 293
napkins, 375, 376, 380
needlepoint, 327
needlework rugs, 254
nylon, 326
    blankets, 379, 380
    floor coverings, 249, 253

oak, 282, 292
olefins, 253, 326
Oriental furnishings, 253, 254, 259, 273, 281, 282
ovenware, 372–373
overdrapery, 334

paint, 256–257, 267, 269
painting, 240, 249–250
paintings, 355, 358
paneling (sheathing), 256, 259, 261, 268
parquet flooring, 240, 250
pattern, use of, 227–228, 229, 235–236, 258, 267, 334
picture frames, 356–358
pictures, 300, 355–359
    hanging, 236, 260, 358–359
pillows, 300, 355
pine, 272
placemats, 375, 380
place settings, 368–369
plants, 360–361
plastics
    dinnerware, 371, 373
    furniture, 273, 282, 287, 290
plate (silver), 366–367
plywood, 250, 256, 259
polyester, 253, 326, 378
pottery, 370–371
printing (fabrics), 329
privacy, window treatments and, 330, 338, 339
provincial style, 277

quilts, 379

rabbet joints, 294
radiators, 275, 309, 324
radios, 394
rattan furniture, 286–287
rayon, 253, 325, 378, 379
registers, warm-air, 309
rosewood, 277, 293